C000150278

LEGACY
SIR GORDON TIETJENS
MY STORY

SIR GORDON TIETJENS is rightly regarded as the greatest sevens coach in history. Under his watch, the New Zealand sevens team became the most successful in the sport, winning four Commonwealth Games gold medals, 12 World Series Sevens titles and two Sevens Rugby World Cups. Renowned for his ability to spot talent, he consistently unearthed future stars, and nurtured the careers of more than 50 All Blacks, including some of the biggest names in the game.

In 2012, Sir Gordon became the first sevens coach to be inducted into the IRB (now World Rugby) Hall of Fame and, in 2013, was knighted for services to the game.

After a remarkable 22 seasons, Sir Gordon stepped down as head coach of the New Zealand sevens team in 2016, following its early exit from the Olympic Games in Rio de Janeiro. He is now coach of the Samoan sevens team.

Sir Gordon is the father of Paul and Kylie and lives in Tauranga with his wife Jules.

LEGACY
SIR GORDON TIETJENS
MY STORY

WITH SCOTTY STEVENSON

PENGUIN BOOKS

CONTENTS

PROLOGUE: Not Like This   6

PART ONE: LAUNCHING A LEGACY

1. Birth of a Salesman   13
2. Building a Profile   25
3. If You Want It, Chase It   37
4. Coaching as a Calling   51
5. Knock, and the Door Will Open   67

PART TWO: UNLEASHING A LEGACY

6. Solid Foundations   83
7. Small Things, Big Difference   99
8. Ground-level Viewing   113
9. Headaches and Medals   125
10. A New Era   137

PART THREE: LEAVING A LEGACY

11. All the Help I Could Get 157

12. Departures and Arrivals 169

13. An Awakening 185

14. Delivering the Goods 199

15. What Goes Up 213

16. So Many Questions 231

17. All She Wrote 245

18. Going Around Again 257

EPILOGUE: On With It 270

By the Numbers 277

Player List 280

Acknowledgements 284

About the Co-author 286

Co-author's Note 287

PROLOGUE
NOT LIKE THIS

'WE'RE NOT THE fucken All Blacks!' That's what I said when I had finally had enough. Then, in an air-conditioned room overlooking a pristine sporting complex on a perfect Florida winter's day, I completely broke down. I had never felt so low in 22 years of coaching sevens, and I was a week out from the biggest event of my life, the 2016 Olympic Games in Rio. For over two decades I had trained players to face life on the breaking point. I had finally found my own line, and taken a step over the edge.

It should have been the greatest experience of my sporting career, and perhaps there was a chance it could still be, but the 18 months leading up to this awkward and confronting meeting in some nondescript office in the middle of the IMG Academy complex in Bradenton had been the most challenging I had ever known. Everything I thought I knew about my ability as a coach, and a manager of people, had come in for questioning. In the time of my greatest need, I had felt deserted. I was now trying to figure out if I still had the support of the very team I was the coach of. It certainly didn't feel that way.

As soon as I had heard that sevens had been included as an Olympic sport I had wanted to be a part of it. In 2009, when the decision had been made, I had already been coach of the New Zealand team for 16 seasons. If I wanted to be in Rio, I still had another six to go. I never once thought that would be a bridge too far. From the moment I had seen my old mate Jonah Lomu celebrating sevens' successful campaign for inclusion, I had my heart set on the chance to coach a team to a gold medal. Now here we were, and we were nowhere near where we needed to be.

I was in the room with Don Tricker, the head of New Zealand Rugby's High Performance team. That morning my side had played a warm-up match against the USA and had been embarrassed. There had been no effort, no precision, no personal standards at all. I had been so devastated to watch them, and was furious with them after the game had finished.

It wasn't that we had lost what was ostensibly a training game, it was the general vibe within the team that had me angry and perplexed. It could have generously – very generously – been described as lacklustre. I couldn't understand why they were so lacking in fizz and pop when the greatest opportunity of their lives was mere days away.

I had spent many months carefully knitting together a plan to win gold and over the last 18 months it felt as if every meticulously crafted stitch had been systematically unpicked. What I had desperately needed from Don and his team was the one thing every coach needs to succeed: playing resources, especially with our escalating injury count. As far as I was concerned, what I had received instead was countless enquiries, and advice that never seemed to match up with what had worked for us for so many seasons. We may have had a name change to share a brand with the All Blacks, but we were the New Zealand Sevens team – a team so fundamentally distinct in size, shape and approach from the national fifteens side that it required a very different way of doing things.

I had honed that approach over 22 years in the job. It was one based on two very simple concepts: culture and conditioning. Everything else – leadership, performance, harmony, respect, pride – flowed out of those two foundation principles. I was tired of hearing what the All Blacks did. As much as I respected that team enormously for its success, it was not the only team in the world that had developed a winning formula. The push to apply their principles across every facet of New Zealand rugby, I believed, was not the magic bullet it was made out to be. Even more ironically, it was, even in this Olympic year, a team that still took precedence over our quest for gold. That had been the cruellest cut of all.

Don was trying to help, I knew that. But when I heard those words again – 'What the All Blacks do is . . .' – I completely lost it. I had never experienced anything like that next few minutes. It was as if someone had sucked all the oxygen from the room and replaced it with a suffocating feeling of helplessness. How had I come to this point? Why did I feel so alone when I had for years considered this team and this game to be my extended family?

I needed to address the players, that much was clear. Shaking off my dismay, I took a deep breath and resolved to find the positives in the pain. The gold medal was still there and it was still up for grabs. If I could just get this ship on the right course there was hope for us yet.

For 22 years I had coached this team based on a simple philosophy that now, more than ever, I had to keep trusting in. It was a philosophy that had been forged from an early age, refined through a successful business career and the pursuit of sporting excellence, and rolled out season after season on some of the finest players ever to take the field. I had learned so much from my players over the years and I had always tried to be positive. Sevens is a sport that does not allow you to dwell on your mistakes or your problems and I wasn't going to do that now. I knew I could still teach them something, too. If they were still willing to listen.

Yes, I wanted them to win a gold medal, but there was no denying I wanted to be able to say I helped them get there. It would top everything else I had achieved as a coach, of that I was certain. Maybe that's why it meant so much to me – it would be the perfect way to finish a coaching career that had developed almost by accident, one which had taken me from a tiny house in Rotorua and was about to deposit me in the very heart of the world's biggest sporting event.

PART ONE

LAUNCHING A LEGACY

1

BIRTH OF A SALESMAN

THE DEFINITION OF a bearing is 'a machine element that constrains relative motion to only the desired motion, and reduces friction between moving parts'. Simply put, it is the part of a machine upon which another part turns or slides, which could also be the perfect definition of 'coach'. Moreover, in that strangely reassuring way life has of coming full circle, my entire coaching career turned on a bearing or, more accurately, on an offer to join a business that made and sold them.

I was destined to be a salesman, or at least that's what my mother, Adeline, always told me. I was the clown of the family, the kid who could talk his way into and, more importantly, out of any situation. I was a prankster with my siblings – older brother Pat, twin brother Gary and younger sister Colleen – and the resident raconteur in the Rotorua railway settlement in which we grew up.

Gary and I had been born in Whanganui where our father was employed as a railwayman. Dad, also Gordon, was a tough, dedicated and conscientious man for whom long shifts and dangerous conditions were a fact of life. He spent many years shunting trains in the yards in Whanganui, several more as a station agent in the tiny King Country settlement of Piriaka, and still more as a guard based in Rotorua, riding the locomotives that ferried stock and timber along the Rotorua branch to the South Waikato town of Putaruru, and beyond to Hamilton and the main trunk line. You could say it was trains, rather than training, which gave me my first inkling of what hard work was.

Like the other railway families, we lived in the railway settlement. Today, Rotorua's Victoria Street is a big-box retail hub, but in the 1960s it was a quiet residential street lined with small timber cottages built by the Railways Department. These houses were, euphemistically speaking, designed under the watch of official railways architect George Troup who was tasked with mass-producing the kitsets out of timber milled from the railways-owned forests.

From the factory at Frankton Junction in Hamilton, Troup and his team made more than 1500 of these prefabricated homes, which were then shipped along the tracks to the various outposts and constructed on site in a matter of weeks. At its peak, the Railways Department boasted more than 6000 houses in its 'fleet'. Even those that weren't designed in the factory shared several common features: they were small, they were cold, and they were cheap.

So it was that our family settled in Rotorua in a three-bedroom timber cottage designed and built in the 1920s. My brothers and I occupied one single room in the house, with Pat comparatively luxuriating on a single bed while Gary and I shared a bunk. Colleen had her own room, as did Mum and Dad, but the kitchen was barely big enough to swing a cat, or a child for that matter, and the toilet, as was the fashion of the time, was located outside.

The winters in Rotorua could be bitterly cold, which added a certain imperative to make sure toilet runs were completed at a clip, and the houses were all heated by the single coal range in the kitchen. On frosty mornings, the mist would mingle with the acrid smoke of coal fires, and thick frosts would blanket the postage-stamp lawns and scruffy kitchen gardens of the quasi-suburban streets.

Once a month I would accompany my father on the coal truck as he made the deliveries to the other houses in the settlement. It was a fact of life for us that you had to do the things that needed to be done before you could do the things you wanted to do. All the kids in the settlement were expected to complete daily and weekly chores, and we were no exception to the rule. It taught us all the value of job satisfaction, and there was never any hint that we would be recompensed in any way for our contributions, other than having fuel for the fire and hot water for the bath.

I mention these things here not to indulge in some Pythonesque reminiscence of youthful suffering, but rather to provide some insight into the personal value system I acquired from a very young age. You had to finish the job before fun could be had. There was, thankfully, plenty of fun. The settlement teemed with children of all ages, meaning a game of rugby, or cricket, or bullrush could break out at a moment's notice. I was never far from the action.

It helped that we were banished from the house on fine afternoons. Mum was a traditional homemaker with a disciplinarian's firm grasp on her young charges. She would not abide us being inside when there was light left in the day, so it was up to us to make our own entertainment well away from whatever was in the oven or from whichever adults were occupying the tiny sitting room. We were expected and encouraged to roam the neighbourhood, knowing full well that the bush telegraph would soon inform our respective parents of any adolescent malfeasance.

We were free-range children, sorting out our own battles, and

My entire coaching career turned on a bearing or, more accurately, on an offer to join a business that made and sold them.

indulging in rough and competitive games wherever and whenever we could. We were tough kids, raised by tough parents, and we soon learned to hold our own when tensions arose. Our fathers never had the time nor the inclination to get entangled in the petty scraps of children, so you either threw the punch or took the punch and that was the end of the matter.

Despite the fact we had very little by way of possessions or spare money, we were always turned out immaculately for school and we were all, above anything else, well versed in being polite and being thankful for all that we did receive. What we received without fail were three square meals a day and a good education, first at St Mary's Convent School a few blocks from our home, then at Rotorua Intermediate School and, finally – at least in the case of my brothers and I, at Rotorua Boys' High School. It was handy that all three schools were within walking distance because we never owned a car.

We never thought it unusual that we didn't possess a conveyance of our own. On top of not having the financial means to purchase a motor vehicle, Dad could never understand why we would want one when we could ride the trains or the New Zealand Road Services buses at a company discount. Besides, our life revolved around just a few square blocks, whether it was for school, for socialising, or for playing rugby on icy mornings on the fields of Arawa Park which spread out towards the lakefront from the end of our street.

I took to rugby from the earliest age, thriving on the contact and the competitiveness, and I embraced those winter Saturdays with all the fervour of a kid for whom Christmas Day came every week. There was nothing I loved more than to get that ball in my hands and run around with my mates, all of us barefooted and revelling in the early morning chill. Rugby was a rite of passage in Rotorua, a proving ground of sorts, and as I came up through the school ranks I obsessed over the sport like nothing else.

By my fourth-form year at Rotorua Boys' High School I was already playing First XV rugby, mainly as a first five-eighth. The games were always rugged, and the rivalries – especially with Western Heights High School, the alma mater of the great All Blacks captain Wayne 'Buck' Shelford – were fierce. Bay of Plenty rugby was steeped in the Maori tradition, with typically uncompromising forward packs and backlines that featured players who boasted wondrous athletic ability and startling vision for any opportunity to attack. When I wasn't playing for school, I would supplement my craving for competitive play with club games, first at Waikite and later at Marist St Michael's from where I would launch my provincial career. Before that, however, I decided to make a radical decision that would ultimately be the making of me as a rugby player: I decided in my final year of school that I wanted to become a loose forward.

I don't know whether it was a dawning realisation that I didn't have the express pace required to achieve representative honours as a back, or whether I just had a burning desire to be more involved in the physical side of the game, but sure enough, I took a single-figure jersey and swapped the backline for the back of the scrum. It would prove, in time and after an exponential increase in bruises and bumps, to be an inspired decision.

Not that everyone was convinced my future was in the forward pack. In my final year of school, I was asked by Marist St Michael's to make my first foray into senior rugby, as a first five-eighth. Impetuousness prevailed and I was more than happy to have a crack despite the protestations of my father who was tough, but not silly. He knew how much more demanding senior club rugby would be than schoolboy play. What he was really trying to say was, 'You'll likely get your young head knocked off.' He was wrong. I got my foot broken instead, in the very first game of the season.

Suitably chastened, and with my hopes of a quick return to play dashed by the doctors, my uncle Dennis thought I might like to try my luck at a trainee programme with a company called International Harvester. Not one to pass up any opportunity, and figuring there wasn't much else to sink my teeth into in Rotorua, I duly packed my bags and headed to Auckland to take up the opportunity at the company's New Zealand headquarters.

International Harvester was a big multinational corporation, manufacturing agricultural equipment, tractors and trucks, and supplying many of the appliances used by the New Zealand Fire Service at the time. It was a complex company, once one of the largest military contractors in the United States, and its complexity – of product, of management and of production lines – meant the trainee programme was an everyday indulgence in intensity and in-depth learning. I loved it, and buried myself in product catalogues and solutions, and the minutiae of the organisation.

I also played rugby, with Marist of course, eventually earning a representative jersey with Auckland as a fourth-grade player and as a Colt (under 21). It would have pleased my father no end that I was playing against lads my own age and size, affording me a lower-percentage chance of suffering mortal injury. The rugby was competitive, and the chance to play a different style of game certainly would prove beneficial upon my return to Rotorua.

The following year I returned home and joined International Harvester full-time. It felt good to be in a paying job after the rigours of the trainee programme, and while I started at the bottom of the ladder, my penchant for curiosity stood me in good stead with the business. Whether it was in the workshop, the spare parts division, or on the road as a sales rep, I found the work challenging and thrived in an environment that rewarded problem solving. I loved the thrill of the chase in sales – still do to this day – and after my stint with the Auckland Colts, I had developed something else: an addiction to competitiveness.

Too often these days, competitiveness is seen as a bad thing, but that is what a life in sport or in business is all about. Unless you are willing to work harder or smarter – or both – than your opposition, you are always going to come second. While International Harvester had the backing of a big global operation, it was hardly the only player in town when it came to the market for that particular type of product. It was beholden to us to be out there grinding as often as we could, to truly understand every aspect of the marketplace and every facet of our customers' business requirements. It was certainly the way I attacked my role, and I was ably assisted in my appetite for success by a bloke who I credit with unlocking what to this day is my pathological distaste for losing.

A lean man with an accountant's head for numbers and a wildly mischievous streak, Tony Dykstra was a costing clerk at International Harvester and also a keen sportsman. Sensing I was on a certain trajectory with my own sporting career, he was only too happy to buddy up when it came to training runs and visits to the gymnasium. Weight training was still in its nascency in the 1970s but, undeterred, Tony and I taught ourselves the various exercises that would soon enough become the staples of the fitness industry. But Tony's influence on me was not restricted to the gym and the running track. That he pushed me in terms of training was a bonus, but I'll forever be more grateful to him for illustrating to me the power of following through on promises and the application to the task that the commercial world demands. The way he would plan his day and his working week was an object lesson in efficiency. Tony also believed firmly in the mantra that the fun can begin once the work has been done.

As much as sales was about the thrill of the chase, it was also about being able to have fun – with workmates, with business acquaintances, and with customers. It was a part of the job – possibly the most important one – to be able to read customers at a personal level as much as a business one. I took great pride in knowing as much as I could about the lives of my clients, looking at all times for a way to interact with them that was more than simply transactional. Rotorua wasn't a big town, and the Bay of Plenty was small enough that bad news spread pretty quickly if you weren't a man of your word. By taking a genuine interest in people, I knew I would be able to open doors that others could not.

As if being a sales rep for International Harvester wasn't enough, I also took up a job selling cars at the local Datsun dealership. I made it my weekend mission to see everyone I knew drive off in a classy 120Y, 120B or 1200S. I had recently bought my first piece of land in Rotorua and I needed the commissions to help pay the mortgage on the property. Again, though, it never hurt to grow your profile, and watching one Sunny after another bunny-hop off the lot certainly helped in that respect.

I enjoyed my time at International Harvester, but as the 1970s ended and the 1980s arrived, the company began to make decisions that would ultimately lead to its downfall as a powerhouse brand. In essence, the business had become obsessed with acquiring assets that shifted its focus further and further away from its core business. The ripple effect was felt in New Zealand which itself was undergoing an economic upheaval of its own. After five years with the firm, and on little more than a hunch, I made the decision to apply for a new role with Swedish bearing giant SKF. It would prove to be one of the smartest things I ever did.

—————

Like International Harvester, SKF was a massive global brand. Its New Zealand operation was already profitable and was looking to grow, thanks in large part to the vision and stewardship of a genial chap named Warwick Talbut. A bespectacled and balding number-cruncher with a restless energy and a big presence that belied his short stature, Warwick was based in Wellington, where I was sent after an initial job interview to be put through the ringer. It remains to this day one of the great grillings of my life, but what was most memorable was the way Warwick was able to anatomise my character with the deftness of a surgeon. He was looking for any sign that I would let him down on the job, any hint that I wouldn't be fully committed to his business. In that single hour, Warwick was able to make the decision that the long-haired, slightly scruffy, rugby-playing salesman in front of him was just the kind of guy who could help grow SKF's business in the Bay of Plenty. For my part, I discovered something much more important: Warwick would become my most cherished personal and career mentor, a second father, and the man who would employ me and advise me for the next 34 years. He was to become my bearing, the point upon which every major part of my career's machinery would turn.

Warwick and I worked closely over the next five years with SKF, after which another opportunity caught his eye. Bay Engineers Supplies was a small family-run business based in Mount Maunganui, part of a rather incongruous industrial hub nestled between the Port of Tauranga harbour and the spectacular strip of white-sand beach that thronged with holidaymakers over the summer months. The company had been in existence since the 1940s and Warwick's expertise had been sought by the owners as they looked to trade their way out of a difficult period. Ever one to take a leap of faith, Warwick had the solution: he bought the business. No sooner had that transaction been completed than he bought something else. That something else was me.

Although I had enormous faith in Warwick's business acumen, the idea of working with him at Bay Engineers was still a risky proposition. He was not the kind of guy to sugar-coat a situation, and he was fairly blunt with regard to his expectations. In short, he was happy to pay me a month's salary. After that it was up to me to be bringing in my own sales income. In all honesty, I didn't exactly have much of a choice. A few weeks earlier, I had been made redundant by SKF. I was resilient enough to know something else would come along, but I was still young enough that I took the decision to heart. Warwick was handing me a lifeline. It was the second time he had decided to take a punt on me, and it wouldn't be the last. As I was to discover from Warwick, and take on board in my work as a coach, the reward for loyalty should always be the freedom to grow. He cultivated that growth in me in ways that could never be imagined then, or repaid now.

2

BUILDING
A PROFILE

IT WASN'T JUST a professional sales career I had embarked upon when I returned to Rotorua after my initial trainee programme with International Harvester. I was keener than ever to rejoin the Marist St Michael's club and give senior rugby a good shot. Buoyed by my time with the Auckland Colts, but still mindful of my father's misgivings about the hurly-burly world of club rugby, I resolved to throw myself into training to put some much-needed bulk on my lean frame. If I was going to mix it with the big boys, I knew I needed to be physical as well as fast.

In the mid-1970s, club rugby was a massive deal all around the country, and the Bay of Plenty was no exception. These were the 'RRB' days of New Zealand manhood: Rugby, Racing and Beer. I wasn't much of a drinker on account of an unfortunate experiment with alcohol a few months earlier in Auckland, and I wasn't much of a gambler either, but I'd be damned if I was going to miss out on the rugby. Marist St Michael's welcomed me home and, weighing in at a paltry 13 stone, I took the field for the first game of the season and never looked back.

Mum was a constant presence on the sideline at those club matches, and would continue throughout her life to be my biggest cheerleader. Dad would come down when he could, but he was less social than Mum and would often wait at home for her full report later in the day. St Michael's was a strong family club, and it was also regarded as the city-slicking club in the Rotorua area, given its proximity to the central business district and the lakefront. That being the case, there were plenty of rivals, all lining up to take the Catholic boys down a peg or two.

There was an imperative placed on uncompromising forward play and there was no shortage of tough-as-teak men who fitted the bill in every sense. I was just 18 years old at the time and frankly in awe of some of the guys I played with and against, but even then, I thought, 'If you're good enough, you're old enough' – a philosophy that I carried with me throughout my playing and coaching career. That season, in 1976, was an absolute eye-opener for me and, given the number of stray fists and elbows and knees I copped during the season, you could say it was an absolute eye-closer as well. It didn't worry me. With each heavy hit that I took and ruck mark I earned across my back, I redoubled my efforts to train harder and to become stronger.

Those efforts did not go unnoticed, and by the conclusion of the club season I had secured my first-ever trial for the Bay of Plenty senior team. I had never played age-group rugby in the blue and yellow hoops, so my selection to trial most certainly raised a few eyebrows. I would ultimately miss out on the final cut, and the team would famously go on to win the inaugural National Provincial Championship title under the captaincy of a rugged and brutal loose forward by the name of Thomas John Waaka. 'Tuck', as he was known to all, came from the Opotiki club and also captained the New Zealand Maori side that year. He was a follow-me kind of guy, and his leadership of that Bay of Plenty side was outstanding.

Waaka left the Bay of Plenty the following year to take up

residency in Northland, where he would continue his representative career with the North Auckland and New Zealand Maori sides. He was a big loss for the province, but his exit undoubtedly opened a door for me. The next season, I was again picked to trial for the provincial side, and this time I was selected. To this day, I still count the feeling of representing the Bay of Plenty for the first time among the very finest I have had. Provincial rugby was a massive deal to us then, and I wish it were still the same. The professional game has altered our relationship with provincial representation, as it is no longer the big deal it once was – or seemed to be – to us.

At the time, everyone in the area knew who was in the provincial side, and I knew that held massive benefits for me in my profession. I was focused on playing the game, but I was also acutely aware of how my growing profile in rugby was helping me on sales calls and in meetings with customers and clients. Suddenly, people weren't dealing with just another salesman, they were dealing with a man who represented them on the rugby field, and that was a powerful tool when you needed to open doors that were tough to open. I have always appreciated the game for the way it brings people together and for how it allows players and supporters to form lifelong bonds. I learned very quickly to appreciate, too, its power to be an unbeatable personal marketing tool.

———

Powerful and personal are probably two words that best describe my first experiences in the Bay of Plenty jersey. My debut would come that year against King Country in Te Kuiti. Home of the famous Meads brothers, Colin and Stan, King Country was still considered a team that was not to be trifled with, lest either one of them got annoyed and came out of retirement! Mum and my brother Gary made the trip for the game, with Gary forced to hire a car as Mum didn't trust his own vehicle to safely convey her to the game and back again. Ever the dutiful son, he did as he was asked and it was a genuine thrill to have them there that day. It was a free-flowing and high-scoring affair, too, and we took the victory 37–20.

That was the powerful part of the story; the personal side of it came a week later against North Auckland at the Tauranga Domain. If there was one particular area of my game, aside from fitness, that I prided myself on, it was my ability to anticipate play. All those years as a youngster playing first five and fullback had taught me a thing or two about the nuances of game management, and I could quickly decipher the tells and shows of most halfbacks and first fives. In rugby, anticipation is a hard skill to coach, but it is one of the most important assets a player can possess. Being able to think ahead – even if just a split second – can be the difference between making and missing the tackle, or seizing the opportunity to attack.

On this particular day, North Auckland's wonderful playmaker Eddie Dunn had decided that the best way to turn us on our heels was to pepper us with pop kicks behind the defensive line. I could sense he was planning on it, and made it my personal mission to corner flag at every opportunity, neatly positioning myself to catch his kicks and diffuse the play. It didn't take long before Eddie tired of my meddling in his game plan. I could tell he was pissed off, though the words he chose to express his annoyance with I will not repeat here. Along with cursing the day of my birth and possibly questioning the integrity of my lineage, he must have also passed a message along to a few of his team-mates. One of them was the All Black Bevan Holmes.

Being able to think ahead – even if just a split second – can be the difference between making and missing the tackle, or seizing the opportunity to attack.

Several minutes later, Holmes decided to pass the message on to me. After I had rushed to a ruck to clear the ball and got the pass away, big Bevan came flying through the melee and clobbered me right in the mush. You could say I got the message. I also got nerve damage in my face, and spent the rest of the season on the sidelines. It was tough to accept that there was no way I would be fit to play for the Bay of Plenty again that year; tougher still to watch as the side was relegated to the second division at the conclusion of the season. Disappointed, and perhaps even feeling slightly aggrieved at my misfortune, I decided to blow town for a while. It would be a decision that set me on a collision course with a future I had never once considered.

***

For many Kiwis, the 'Big OE' is a rite of passage. Every year, thousands of youngsters board planes, fly to London, and spend the next year or two dossing on couches, drinking their body weight weekly in bitter ales, and finding enough work to pay for side trips to Europe until it is time to head home and maybe get serious about a career. Several friends had already exercised this option and, given the local rugby season was over, I figured it wouldn't hurt to join them. It was an impetuous move on my part, and not a popular one with my family in whose conservative eyes this was out of character, even for the resident joker in the pack. I would not be dissuaded (stubbornness, as you will come to learn, is my cross to bear) and so it was that for the first time in my life I left the country and ventured abroad.

It was not all it was cracked up to be. Don't get me wrong, I certainly enjoyed the company of friends and some wonderful experiences travelling through the European mainland, but London in the 1970s was a rough place, cold and grey over those long winter months, and the work I was able to get was generally low-paid. Fortunately, there was rugby, and no sooner had I dropped the bags at my newfound flat than I was off to find a club to play for. That club was London Welsh. Formed in 1885, London Welsh had a long-standing connection with both Welsh rugby and the English championship. Throughout the 1960s and 1970s the club was considered one of the strongest in British rugby, winning six English and two Welsh club titles during this period. It was famed for producing Welsh internationals, and had also supplied a record seven players for the famous 1971 British Lions team that toured New Zealand: John Dawes, J. P. R. Williams, Gerald Davies, Melvyn Davies, John Taylor, Mike Roberts and Geoff Evans.

Although I thought I was a fairly handy player, London Welsh weren't about to offer me a spot in the top team on a New Zealand reputation. First, I was selected for their Third XV, then the following week I moved up to the second team. I must have been going alright because by the third week I was selected for the top side, and my first taste of televised Anglo-Welsh club rugby. Our opponent that day was the famous Welsh club Llanelli – which had defeated the All Blacks at the windswept Stradey Park back in 1972. They were still celebrating five years later. We had home advantage for this clash, played at Old Deer Park in Richmond in front of a crowd of around 10,000. I was a replacement that day, but my chance to take the field would come when Richard Thomas tore his shoulder trying to bash his way through the Llanelli pack and came off second best. Those big Welsh forwards were bludgeoning, brutal men with a bloodlust for contact and a determination to tackle and maul and ruck their way through anything in front of them. I was accustomed to physical play, but no sooner had I reckoned that I was finding my feet than they quite literally went out from beneath me. I performed what might generously be called a full split, tore my groin, and was stretchered off the park.

It seemed grossly unfair to have had two club seasons in the same year effectively ruined by injury, but I didn't want to mope my way through the rest of my overseas trip. I vowed to recover quickly and get myself fit again for play, no matter what shape that would eventually take. What regular work I did have was as a result of club connections and I didn't want to let that slide. I had already learned that rugby was a great way to meet people and to gain opportunities. If I put in the effort, more opportunities would follow, and if I knew which opportunities to take, success would follow those. It's a philosophy that has never left me, not once, in my playing, coaching or business life. If you are prepared to work, the rewards will come.

Fundamentally, it was for that reason that I found myself fit and ready for action as the English sevens season rolled around. I had no idea about sevens, had rarely if ever played the game in New Zealand, and hadn't the first clue about how the positional set-up worked. What I did know was that I was fit, I was keen, and I was champing at the bit to get back on a rugby field. You could say I fell for the game's charms almost immediately. Here was a game that placed priority on pace and space rather than bulk and savagery. It was action from the first whistle to the last, a lung-busting 14 minutes of genuine effort with and without the ball, all played out in front of raucous crowds and in a wonderful collegial spirit.

Putting my hand up for sevens was undoubtedly one of the best things I did in my time in England. My deeds for London Welsh in those few weeks gained the attention of one of the most successful sevens clubs of all, Richmond, and I enjoyed further tournament exposure with them as the season wound down. It was a wonderful, fulfilling experience to find a sport that matched my particular strengths as a player: speed, fitness and anticipation. It was a fast game and I ran a lot, trained a lot, and had that anticipation. Sevens not only opened my eyes to all-new possibilities in rugby, it also very much replenished my desire to see how far a playing career could take me. First things first, though, I needed to get home. I was tired of living off small means in a smaller flat, and had a fledgling career to return to in Rotorua, thanks to International Harvester holding a job for me while I took the opportunity to broaden my horizons. With a valedictory tour of France to finish my sojourn, I boarded the plane in Heathrow and, like so many Kiwis before and since, returned to New Zealand with little money, many fond memories, and the travel bug sated for the time being.

Sometimes the best training is not vocational, but rather about learning how to survive and thrive in a completely different environment. When I returned to the Bay of Plenty I was wiser, more self-confident, and hungrier than ever to make my mark both in work and in sport. Sevens, naturally, would play a big part in what was to come, although fifteens again became my primary focus in the meantime. Having had a taste of provincial representation, I was eager for more and I had my share of opportunities over the final years of the 1970s and into the early 1980s. I also had my share of selection frustrations over that period, often feeling aggrieved at being named on the bench, or at being left out of the playing side altogether. I was, naturally, fiercely competitive and wanted to play as much as I could, so in many ways I look back on this period as a tough but important lesson: if you don't get picked, don't give up.

Midway through the 1981 season, after being left out of the side for three straight weeks, a period that included a Ranfurly Shield challenge against Waikato, I was picked once more to start for the Bay of Plenty. I was thrilled to be back in the mix, playing number eight with the impressive Kevin Eveleigh and the raw and dynamic Frank Shelford as my loose forward partners. Much has been written of the ill-fated South African tour to New Zealand that year, a tour dubbed 'a war played out twice a week'. It was the most divisive event in New Zealand sporting history, and the nation was torn between a love for rugby and a growing awareness of the power of its moral conscience in opposition to the apartheid regime. No one who lived through that time would question its impact on us as a country. Friendships were tested, families were split, people were hurt badly, and rugby as a sport would take many seasons to recover from those turbulent and tumultuous 56 days. Rotorua would have its turn to host the visiting side on 2 September, just four days after the Springboks had levelled the test series with the All Blacks in Wellington. I was named to play in the game.

There is no doubt that many players across the country wrestled internally with the prospect of playing a tour match against that Springbok side. Already games in Hamilton and Timaru had been cancelled due to protests and security fears, and we had all watched the scenes in Wellington the weekend before Bay of Plenty's scheduled meeting, as protesters, police and fans clashed outside Athletic Park. There was a surrealistic quality to those sights that still seems fresh in the mind – the batons, the blood, the police lines busting through the protests and shepherding fans into the match. A few days earlier, protesters had occupied the runway at Rotorua Airport in an attempt to prevent the Springboks from landing. Local iwi also voiced their displeasure, refusing to host the visitors on marae, and not allowing them to set foot on the famed Whakarewarewa thermal grounds. But we wanted our shot at playing that team, and we buried all thoughts of what may happen around us under a solemn vow to give the Springboks a game to remember. We certainly didn't disappoint.

I will never forget the feeling of running out onto Rotorua Stadium that day with the stands packed and the massive grass banks a sea of colour and a cacophony of sound. The game was as physical and frenetic as we all expected it to be and despite extending a hard-fought halftime lead to 21–13 midway through the second spell, we were eventually caught and overtaken by the visitors. I did have one last chance to win the game, after charging down a clearing kick in the final moments. Unfortunately, the bounce of the ball did me in, the Springboks forced for the 22 drop-out, and they held on to win the game 29–24.

Despite everything that was going on around that tour, I don't think I had ever played a better 80 minutes in my young career, or enjoyed a game more. I was awarded the man of the match honours at the after-match function, which didn't exactly erase the pain of losing, but did go some way towards making me feel like I belonged at that level. It was certainly a performance that was noted in the area, and I believed that only strengthened my standing within the community, especially when my job centred on calling on clients and building those networks. I regarded that game as something of a personal breakthrough, a way to really announce my arrival on the scene. Turns out that just when you think you've made it, life has a funny way of bringing you back down to earth.

3

IF YOU WANT IT, CHASE IT

I LOVED THE thrill of the chase and the joy of the catch. In many ways, that was why I found sales so attractive. It was a career that required self-motivation and the willingness to go out and seek opportunities, wherever they lay. Sales wasn't about being handed a job to do; it was about finding the job, fulfilling the requirements, and making sure you quickly moved on to the next piece of business. There was no room for complacency, and no point in waiting around for clients to fall into your lap. I loved the relentless nature of the role, and the way it forced me to be resourceful, and hungry, on a daily basis.

When Warwick Talbut asked me to move with him to Bay Engineers in 1983, after I had been made redundant by SKF, I had faced a big blow to my self-confidence. I'd had a similar feeling the year before with Bay of Plenty rugby, when I had originally missed out on the 1982 team, only to earn a late reprieve and be called back into the squad. Undoubtedly, I took both those rejections hard at the time, but I vowed to press on, both with Warwick in his new enterprise and with Bay of Plenty under coach Graeme Crossman, with whom I enjoyed a rather fraught relationship. I felt my predilection for practical jokes – often at his expense – had greatly affected his belief in me as a player. Graeme would later reject that claim, instead pointing to the quality of loose forwards available for selection as the real reason I was somewhat down the pecking order. He was certainly right about the calibre of players at his disposal. Kevin Eveleigh, Frank Shelford and Graeme Elvin were a formidable trio and they fronted for the side in most of the games that season. All up, I managed just five appearances for Bay that year, during which the side won just one of its first-division fixtures and avoided relegation only by virtue of a win against Taranaki, who were eyeing up their own elevation to the top flight of the provincial championship. The following year, after yet another rejection, I decided to take my destiny into my own hands.

———

Ever since my return from England I had taken it upon myself to learn as much as I could about the game of sevens. I was the chief agitator for St Michael's at club level and would press-gang anyone I could find into sevens service whenever the chance to play a tournament presented itself. Club tournaments weren't exactly common, and at the provincial level sevens had very little profile at all. Although an annual national provincial tournament had been held since 1975, most unions didn't see it as a priority, and neither did *The Rugby Almanack of New Zealand*, which for many years did not devote a single sentence to the event.

Regardless, the national event was beginning to garner greater interest from the unions and the players, in part because of an international invitational tournament that had sprung to life a few years earlier in the most unlikely place: Hong Kong. The Hong Kong Sevens was – quite literally – a case of the smoke before the fire. It was a concept developed by the then chairman of the Hong

Kong Rugby Football Union, A. D. C. 'Tokkie' Smith, in response to a sponsorship offer from Ian Gow, a tobacco company executive who was keen to find a rugby property to support and to no doubt emblazon with his particular brand of cigarettes. Smith, with wonderful prescience born of pragmatism, suggested sevens rather than fifteens, which would make it easier for the various invitees to find and field teams. It was a masterstroke of management and, in 1976, the tournament that would become the most famous of its kind kicked off.

Such was the standing of sevens in those days that the New Zealand Rugby Football Union (NZRFU) did not see the value in selecting or sending a national side to what they obviously perceived as little more than a marketing sideshow. They were not alone. In fact, in the first seven years of the tournament, Australia would be the only one of the traditional rugby powerhouses to send a national side. Amazingly, the Welsh would not do so until 1990, Scotland would only follow suit the next year, Ireland two years after that, and England, ever the stick-in-the-mud, would first participate under the national banner in 1995. New Zealand had been invited to the very first tournament but had opted to send a Cantabrians side, featuring members of the Marlborough team that had won the first two National Sevens championships in 1975 and 1976. The Cantabrians were duly crowned inaugural winners, and the union seemed confident that, from then on, the best provincial team in New Zealand would be more than capable of representing New Zealand on their behalf. What they did not count on was the sevens pedigree of a tiny island neighbour, and the willingness of the tournament organisers to stand up for the integrity of the event.

In 1977, Fiji won its very first Hong Kong Sevens, and the

following year, with the tournament expanding from 12 to 16 teams, it claimed its second consecutive championship. On both occasions, Fiji defeated New Zealand's provincial representatives, Marlborough and Manawatu respectively, in the final. It was clear that the Fijians were preternaturally gifted at sevens rugby, and they fast became the darlings of the tournament, claiming a third title a couple of years later, in 1980. New Zealand's teams, meanwhile, did not fare so well and in 1982 the tournament organisers handed the New Zealand union an ultimatum: send a national side, or don't bother coming. Needless to say, no team left New Zealand shores. Australia, led by John Maxwell and a youthful David Campese, would go on to win the 1982 title, and the following year the New Zealand union acquiesced to the tournament's demands. It was decided that in 1983, for the first time, a national side would represent New Zealand at the Hong Kong Sevens. That was more than enough motivation for me, and I duly lined up for the Bay of Plenty trials that year, eager to get myself into the mix, by hook or by crook, for selection. The side would have to go through a qualifying tournament in Pukekohe in order to make the nationals in Feilding, and I was ready to do my part to get us through. Unfortunately, my enthusiasm for the game was not enough for Graeme Crossman, and I was once again left disappointed when the team was announced.

I have learned in life that desire is a weapon we all can wield and, if it burns strongly enough within you, no one can ever extinguish that flame. In other words, if you have the will, you can find the way. What I found was the phone number for George Simpkin, the Waikato coach, and I immediately set about dialling it. I did not want to turn my back on my province, but if I couldn't win a spot in the Bay of Plenty side, I would never discover how far I could go in sevens. Waikato had already qualified for the national tournament, they were our neighbouring province, and they just might have a spot available.

George Simpkin was an incredibly insightful rugby coach and a very deep thinker on the game. He had been just 22 years old when he started coaching at his Matamata United club in 1966, and had held the Waikato job since 1976, leading them to a Ranfurly Shield win against Auckland in 1980. He was a lean man with an intense stare and a forceful manner that betrayed his school-teaching background, and he loved innovation above all else. His eye for opportunity and keen sense of adventure would eventually see him go on to coach in some of the most unexpected places in the rugby world, including Sri Lanka, China, Germany and Hong Kong. Somewhat surprised by my call, George informed me that the Waikato side had already been picked. I was devastated; I had no Plan C. For the next few days, I wracked my brain to think of another way to get myself into the frame for the nationals, but each idea seemed more fanciful than the last.

Just as had I resigned myself to the fact that I would simply have to wait another year, the telephone rang. It was George Simpkin again. Miah Melsom, the Waikato flanker, had suffered an injury and the team needed a replacement. Would I still be keen? I had barely finished answering in the affirmative, when George laid down the catch: I would have to make myself available for the Waikato fifteens side in that year's provincial championship. It was a massive decision to make. On the one hand, I was being given a fantastic opportunity – the opportunity I had craved. On the other, I was being asked to turn my back on Bay of Plenty and align myself with an arch-rival, not just for the sevens tournament, but for the entire season. I knew in my heart what I wanted to do. More importantly, I knew in my gut what I had to do. That gut instinct would serve me well throughout my life, and right then it was telling me to grab my chance with both hands. It was telling me to chase my goals.

———

Club rugby may not be such a big deal in the modern professional landscape, but I can assure you, at that particular time, it most certainly was. My club, St Michael's, was very supportive of my decision but certainly made their dim view of my non-selection for Bay of Plenty well known among the club and provincial devotees of the day. I was grateful that they backed me in my quest – it gave credence to my instinctive decision, and also gave me a certain amount of comfort knowing that I would always be welcome back there if and when the time arose to return.

And so it was that I registered immediately with the Putaruru rugby club, ensuring my eligibility for Waikato selection, rendezvoused there with the team minivan, and headed to Feilding for the nationals, where I would have my first and last training run with the team in a hotel carpark on the morning of the tournament. It had been a whirlwind few days, to say the least, but once we arrived at the park all of the upheaval of the past week was forgotten. I was where I wanted to be and was ready to play. I didn't get the chance to cross paths with the Bay of Plenty side. They had been knocked out of the qualifying tournament and failed to make the national event.

I have learned in life that desire is a weapon we all can wield and, if it burns strongly enough within you, no one can ever extinguish that flame.

It was a sensational tournament to be a part of and though I didn't play in the first two matches, George Simpkin finally gave me a shot in the third. We were behind, and by some distance, against Counties when I finally got my chance to take the field, but we managed to claw our way back into the match and eventually get the victory. I was able to score a couple of tries in that game, doing enough in George's eyes to earn a starting spot against Auckland in the final. It was a cracking match – fast, furious and intense right from the first kick-off. In the end, Auckland came away with a one-point victory, but we were proud of our effort and satisfied that we had given our all for the cause.

Showered and changed, we gathered for the post-tournament function to swap stories from the day, enjoy a few well-earned refreshments, and see who had been picked for the New Zealand team. Bryce Rope, the chairman of the New Zealand selectors, eventually took the floor. Working in alphabetical order, Bryce began to read out the names: 'Alan Dawson, Counties, Captain; Andy Donald, Wanganui; Richard Fry, Auckland; Ken Granger, Manawatu; Allan Lindsay, Canterbury; Hika Reid, Bay of Plenty; Glenn Rich, Auckland . . .' I wasn't genuinely expecting to hear my name, but I was secretly counting the number of players on my hands while simultaneously working my way through the alphabet in my mind. Bryce continued to read out names while I mentally multi-tasked: 'Bruce Smith, Waikato; Joe Stanley, Auckland . . .' Surely that was that, I remember thinking, and then I heard one more name: 'Gordon Tietjens, Waikato.'

It took a few seconds to register that the final name was mine. It didn't quite sound right to hear 'Waikato' in the same breath as 'Gordon Tietjens'. Hell, I had been a Waikato player for all of one and a half games of sevens! Still, I was not mistaken – I had been selected for the New Zealand Sevens team!

I would never forget what it felt like to hear my name called out to represent my country. Not that I knew it at the time, but a decade later I would get my first chance to name players in a New Zealand side myself. On that occasion, and on every occasion after it, I would think of that day in Feilding, with my partner and my mum there to share with me what was the most cherished and special moment I could possibly have imagined as a player. That was all in some unimagined future, however, and for now I was going to Hong Kong, to play sevens for New Zealand, and I couldn't wait to get on that plane and take the field once more.

Hong Kong is a city that assaults the senses like no other. Even before we arrived, we were subjected to the famous Kai Tak Airport approach, a one-of-a-kind landing manoeuvre during which pilots were forced to fly directly towards a mountainside before making a dramatic, late, right-hand turn while simultaneously taking the plane down at a steep angle, mere metres above the rooftops of Kowloon, to finally land on the short runway that jutted out into the brown waters of the bay. It had thrilled and terrified passengers and pilots alike since 1925, and I was definitely feeling a dizzying mixture of both as we touched down for our first foray into the Hong Kong Sevens.

Bryce Rope was our coach on the trip and what he knew about sevens could probably have been written on the end of a chopstick. Admittedly, there wasn't an awful lot of sevens experience in the team, purely because sevens had never been a major deal in New Zealand rugby. None of this seemed to be of concern to any of us as we set about training among the apartment buildings and the noise and unfamiliar sights and sounds of that amazing city. While there was little by way of sevens-specific guidance, we understood we had an obligation to the jersey and we backed ourselves to go out there and uphold the traditions of New Zealand rugby, regardless of how little experience we boasted as a collective.

We also knew that as the first New Zealand representative team there would be an enormous amount of pressure on us to perform. You can never shy away from that expectation, as I would come to learn in later years. Expectation is the catalyst for preparation, and harnessed properly it is a powerful tool that the most successful teams learn to master, wielding it with an artful precision to craft their success. Given we were charting new territory on that trip, it was not surprising that we perhaps hadn't quite got our heads around how to productively combine expectation and preparation. We also had something else to contend with. Turns out, when it rains in Hong Kong, it pours. It would be fair to say that conditions at the tournament were nothing short of monsoonal. I doubt any of us had ever played in conditions as bad. It rained without cease on the sodden pitch of the Government Stadium in So Kon Po, and it also rained on our parade. We were undefeated in pool play as we took down such teams as Bahrain, South Korea, Singapore and the United States, but in the quarterfinals we were tipped up by Western Samoa. So much for our hopes of returning to New Zealand triumphantly.

Not making the top four of the tournament was an incredible disappointment for all of us and I was personally left smarting after only having had one outing on the field, against Singapore. All that was left was to sit back and watch the finals as Australia went through to win their second consecutive title in front of a boisterous, if somewhat saturated, crowd. It would not be until 1986 that a New Zealand team would be crowned champions of Hong Kong, sparking an enduring and cherished rivalry with Fiji that to this day has a defining influence on the season fortunes of both sides. That would all be after my time as a player. That one tournament was my first and last opportunity to represent my country on the field.

———————

I returned to New Zealand intent upon honouring my word to George Simpkin, and at the conclusion of the club season I was selected to represent the Mooloo men in the National Provincial Championship. It was an enjoyable time and I managed to play in 14 games, including a midweek fixture against the touring British Lions. Undoubtedly, it was an invaluable experience to play for a team that had a distinctly different style to what I was used to in the Bay of Plenty. George was a coach who was always on the hunt for new ways to do things, adjusting tactics to unsettle opposition teams, and searching constantly for alternative strategies to unpick defences or to spark attacks. It didn't always work that year, but it gave me a great insight into a genuine coaching mind.

Coaching, of course, was nowhere on my radar at this time. I still had aspirations as a player and, more importantly in that amateur age, I was working hard to help Warwick Talbut build his business. When he had brought me on board that year it was on the proviso that I would back myself to bring in enough income to justify my position. Put another way, if I couldn't make it pay, I would soon be looking for alternative employment. Warwick was unbelievably supportive when it came to my rugby and my quest for that shot at the New Zealand team, but he had a company to run and I was expected to pull my weight on the sales front. Loyalty is not blind, and Warwick's eye was keen. I knew that and accepted it, and vowed to never let my work ethic fail either me or him.

With business growing and a committed relationship to attend to, at the conclusion of that 1983 domestic season I made the decision to return home and once again play my rugby in the Bay. I knew St Michael's would welcome me home – they had made that clear once I had made the call to sign up with Waikato for sevens – but it was time to make another move, this time to Tauranga where I could be better placed to serve Bay Engineers' growing customer base. I played the season with the Mount Maunganui club and was reselected for the Bay of Plenty side that year. I would continue to earn selection for Bay of Plenty for the next four seasons alongside many fine men who would go on to earn higher honours and distinguish themselves as outstanding provincial players. I look back now at mentions in *The Rugby Almanack of New Zealand* with a chuckle. In the 1985 edition it was noted that Craig Burrell and I were 'useful loose forwards'. In the 1986 edition, I 'was always busy'. In 1987, it was written that I had 'helped the team out of trouble time and time again'.

The 1987 season, however, would be my last for the Bay of Plenty. After 81 games, and at the age of 30, I decided to call time on my playing career. I was proud of what I had achieved, and still am to this day. I had gone after a representative career and I had achieved my goal. I had chased and I had caught. Perhaps if I had one regret, it was not playing 100 games for the union, but that's small beer in the scheme of things. I think back on those last few *Almanack* entries. 'A useful loose forward who was always busy and who helped his team out of trouble time and time again' doesn't sound like a bad valediction, to be honest. In fact, it sums up just the kind of player I would look for as a coach. And soon enough, I would get that chance.

4

COACHING AS A CALLING

EVERY ONE OF us needs to ensure we have a challenge to look forward to each day. For me, for as long as I could remember, playing rugby had provided me with that challenge. Every training run, every visit to the gym, every freezing winter weekend, was either endured or anticipated because I knew that I would be running out for my club, or for my province, and I was there to do what I could to help the team win. When I finished my playing career, I realised very quickly that I needed another challenge. I needed to reassess my 'why'.

I was never one for whom 'just because' was an adequate answer. It wasn't in the Tietjens DNA to shrug the shoulders and accept anything at face value. Although we had all chosen different career paths, my brothers, Pat and Gary, and I were all strangely similar in one respect: we had chosen jobs that were all based around pulling things apart. In the case of Pat, who had left school to become a mechanic, and me, we also enjoyed reassembling those constituent parts, albeit in a way that made them work better than before. Gary, from the age of 15, had chosen butchery – a trade he would specialise in for his entire life. In fairness, Gary didn't often put things back together once he had pulled them apart – unless you count his fine sausages, that is. It may have been our father's influence. Dad's job on the railways was a complicated one, involving many moving parts – both from a physical perspective, and from a scheduling point of view. Dad spent his life making sure each part of the process worked, whether he was shunting trucks around the yard, or riding the trains on the branch lines. It was his responsibility to make sure all of those parts fitted together, when they needed to and how they needed to. I guess that part of his mind, if you'll excuse the pun, was passed down to all of us, our sister Colleen included.

So, over the next couple of years, I filled with work the space in my life that playing rugby used to fill. When I had started with Warwick, we had set ourselves the initial, simple challenge of bringing in enough business in the first month to ensure there was money to keep me in employment after that. We had set about achieving that aim with a certain necessary gusto, and after reaching our initial targets we had continued to set our aims higher and higher. That was the way we had managed to grow the company's footprint across the Bay and the wider region; and as we had grown, so had our workforce. As we developed our brand and our business strategy, and employed more people, I leaned heavily on that early work experience with International Harvester, where I had been trained in all areas of the business. It was where I had first honed that hunger to learn everything I could about the company I worked for and the products we sold and serviced. Every single scintilla of information I could soak up would invariably be of assistance to me on the road as I went about my sales calls.

Once I had built that knowledge of the business, and of the customers' businesses, I could use that to construct a compelling pitch, or to more effectively discuss problems and solutions with the people I was calling on. That knowledge leads to trust, and that trust leads to lasting and mutually respectful relationships. My rugby career had certainly helped me open doors, but it was my desire to truly understand what I was there to do and how I would go about doing it that got me the seat and the cup of tea. It was a strength of mine to figure out who I needed to talk to. Who was the key decision-maker or was there more than one in a particular enterprise? In most cases, big decisions are made by a number of people, so you have to become adept at selling your message to several people at once. Even when you think you have the best idea, you're still going to have to get that crucial buy-in. That can be tough. As the former Clerk of the House of Commons, Sir Barnett Cocks, once said: 'A committee is a cul-de-sac down which ideas are lured and then quietly strangled.' As much as I love that line (and as much truth as it ultimately contains), I was never one to be dissuaded. The more people I needed to convince, the stronger my resolve would be.

As the business grew, I realised I had another set of people I needed to build a productive relationship with: our own staff. From being singularly focused on my own accounts, I now found that with each passing day I was beginning to have a greater influence on the staff around me – whether it was the simple act of offering some advice on a particular customer, imparting a piece of knowledge on a product line, or assisting in crafting tender documents or budget plans. I came to see that the same analytical thinking that I had applied externally to sell our business could also be harnessed internally to improve our business. In short, I was beginning to understand how to teach. More accurately, I was beginning to understand how to coach.

There was another new drive in my life as well. In March 1988, Glenys and I had welcomed our first child, Paul, into the world.

It would have been the ideal time to channel my energies into work and fatherhood, yet there was still something missing. As much as I had moved on from playing the game of rugby, I missed the camaraderie and the involvement in the game I loved. I kept thinking about a letter written to me by the St Michael's club committee when I had made the decision to leave Bay of Plenty rugby back in 1983. In it, they had expressed their hope that I would one day return to the club 'so that the young players coming up may benefit from your experience and knowledge'. While I couldn't repay the club at that time, I knew instinctively that I should give coaching a go. In 1991 I applied for, and was given, the role of Colts coach for the Bay of Plenty. I hadn't exactly formulated a plan of attack in terms of how I would approach the job, but if my playing career had taught me anything, it was to go after the things you wanted most. If I wanted to coach, this was my opportunity to do so. Why pass it up? I was grateful to be given that chance and, from the moment I stepped out for my first training run with the team, I knew two things: I was going to love every second of coaching, and I needed to learn all I could as fast as I could.

―――――――

In essence, coaching is nothing more than a straightforward transfer of information. If you don't have that information, you can't ever hope to pass it on. Conversely, there are coaches who have an enormous amount of knowledge but lack the ability to transfer it, either because they lack the teaching instinct, or because they don't command respect. I was aware very early on that every successful coach had one common trait: they had a presence that commanded respect. That presence could manifest in many different ways –

emotionally, physically, or intellectually – but it had to be there. My playing history certainly helped in terms of having a ready-built reputation. The players in the Colts system were old enough to remember at least a part of my provincial career, so from that point of view I didn't have to explain my rugby credentials to them. I was intent, however, on making sure I had the coaching knowledge as well as the playing knowledge. What could I focus on immediately as I broadened my skills in the technicalities of the craft? The answer was the one thing I would go on to be known for more than anything else: fitness.

While rugby had given me the perfect reason to enhance and perfect my approach to fitness, it was a very different sport that had first opened my eyes to its ultimate importance. When I had been a student at Rotorua Boys' High School, intervals and lunchtimes were reserved for sports. Whatever the season, if the sun was shining, there was some form of hastily organised game to be enjoyed with groups large or small. In summer months, it was a strange hybrid game of tennis played on the school courts. I needed no second invitation to play, but I didn't stop there. I had to teach myself how to play tennis properly. I had no coach and no formal training, but I had a bucket of tennis balls, access to a court, and a desire for self-improvement. Eventually I would join the Rotorua Lawn Tennis Club where I came to the attention of a man by the name of Ron Mahy, the cousin of the late internationally celebrated children's author Margaret Mahy. What Margaret was to kids' books, Ron was to kids' tennis – certainly in the Bay of Plenty – and it was he who deserves the credit for giving me my first genuine insights into fitness training, insights I carried with me as a player and then as a coach.

Ron, who sadly passed away in 2013, was a great player in

his own right, a man who could hit a double-handed backhand before it was fashionable. I used to spend hours trying to imitate that shot, and must admit I never once mastered it. As much as Ron enjoyed a certain amount of flamboyance in the play of his charges, he demanded fitness above all else. His training runs were brutal, an energy- and spirit-sapping menu of 400-metre sprints and shuttle runs. And more shuttle runs. Many was the session during which the racquets were not even taken from the bag. As much as these training days hurt like hell, the fact was they had the desired results. Technically I wasn't the greatest player, but I won more matches than I should have on pure fitness alone. Tennis is a game of repetition, and in Ron's eyes running was as much a part of that repetitive regime as anything else. In my case, being supremely fit was as much about on-court survival as anything else. My backhand was my weakest shot and as such I preferred to run around the ball in order to use my forehand. That added many more cumulative steps to my workload in every match, and I simply would not have been able to compete had I not developed a discipline around training, and around Ron's fitness regime. Under Ron, not only did I compete, but I rose to become the top-ranked junior in the Bay of Plenty.

I learned to love tournament play as a youngster, and relished the opportunity to play against juniors from other regions. I once even entered a Maori tennis tournament in Rotorua, even though I certainly had no right to! I blame my childhood friend Greg Johnson for that. He at least was Maori, which made me feel better when we joined forces in the doubles draw. Fortunately, I was knocked out in the quarterfinals. I think my fear of being exposed as a fraud probably undid me more than my backhand did on that particular occasion.

As much as I enjoyed tennis – and would continue to play throughout my adult life – any aspirations I had of really making something of a career out of it were shattered one evening in Auckland, where I had travelled to play a night tournament. I had made it through to the third round of the event when I came up against a long-haired kid who took one look at me, chuckled a little, and proceeded to demolish me 9–1 without even taking his tracksuit top off. I knew then that I was never going to turn pro, and headed back to Rotorua with my tail between my legs. Some years later, in 1983, I would represent my country in sevens while that same kid – Chris Lewis – would become just the second New Zealander, and the seventh unseeded man, to reach a Wimbledon final. He would face John McEnroe and ultimately be defeated in straight sets. I remember watching that match and feeling rather amazed that we had ever shared the same court.

What Ron Mahy had taught me in tennis, I now passed on to my players in rugby. It was fitness first from the day I stepped into a coaching role with the Bay. I was greatly assisted by a big, bruising kid called Clayton McMillan who was my first captain in the Colts. Clayton was a man who would run through a brick wall if you asked him to. Naturally quiet, he had an oversized presence that, much like a planet's gravitational force, pulled players towards him. He was a wonderful trainer with a deeply entrenched work ethic, and he put an incredible effort into those early training sessions, leading his team through his actions, and validating my focus on fitness above all else. Clayton would go on to play in the senior Bay of Plenty side and collect more than 100 caps for the province. He would later go on to coach the Steamers, as they became known, and also to coach the New Zealand Provincial Barbarians side against the touring British and Irish Lions in 2017. He was just the kind of player I admired: tireless, tenacious, and willing to put every last ounce of his effort into each game he played.

Coaching was both cathartic and energising for me. It gave me a sense of purpose outside family and work commitments, and nourished my appetite for learning and for knowledge. In coaching, as in business, you are constantly tasked with analysing opponents, devising strategies and tactics, and searching for the right solutions. Every week, there were more questions than answers, which naturally fed my innate curiosity. The central question was always the same: How could I dismantle the constituent parts of the team or the performance and reassemble them in a way that achieved a more desirable outcome? I threw myself at the task, consulting widely to fill in the gaps, putting myself forward as a resource coach for the NZRFU and attending every course I could find. It was during this time that I met many people whose wisdom and tutoring I would come to greatly appreciate as my career developed. And it would develop more rapidly than I could have ever expected. After just one year with the Colts, I was asked to apply for the position of head coach of the senior provincial side. I duly applied, and was appointed. It would be a major step up in terms of pressure, and a lesson in the harsh realities of first-class coaching.

Bay of Plenty had been relegated to second-division rugby at the conclusion of the 1991 National Provincial Championship after suffering defeat to King Country in the promotion/relegation match. It was the first time since 1977 that the side had taken the drop, and the union was desperate to get back into the top flight

In coaching, as in business, you are constantly tasked with analysing opponents, devising strategies and tactics, and searching for the right solutions.

of the domestic competition as soon as possible. I knew that they expected results, but I was very clear in my interview that I thought it would take time. In my opinion, it was going to require four or five years to reclaim a spot in the first division. It wasn't just a guess. I could see that Bay of Plenty was caught between two generations – one of players who were nearing the end of their careers and who carried with them experience but not form, and one of youngsters who had plenty of potential but none of the experience that was vital to the team's chances of success. I believed that I would have to manage that transition, and that it was one that was unlikely to bear fruit early. I hoped pragmatism would trump parochialism, and it seemed the board agreed. I was appointed to the job, replacing John Brake, and decided on a course of action that would ultimately set me off on a coaching career path I could not possibly have imagined. I decided to enter a Bay of Plenty side in the Melrose Sevens in Scotland.

When it comes to sevens rugby, Melrose is officially the big bang, the very origin of the game from which its ever-expanding universe can be traced back to. The tournament itself was the brainchild of a local butcher and Melrose RFC player, Ned Haig, who in 1883, while searching for ways to raise much-needed funds for the club, struck upon the idea of an abbreviated version of the game that would attract a number of visiting teams, and presumably a paying crowd, for a day-long tournament at the club's home, The Greenyards, in the Scottish Borders. Haig's concept was a runaway success, and since that day, with the exception of the time of the two world wars, the tournament has been held every year.

The trip to Melrose was in many ways experimental. Certainly, we were going there to do as well as we could, but I wanted to give some of the younger guys in the team a chance to shine away from the pressure of fifteens. More than that, I wanted to take with me a team that looked like a sevens team. It had become clear to me in the years since I had played sevens that the game required a different type of athlete, one who had a different kind of awareness and vision. I had been mulling over this theory for some time, and now I had a chance to test it in a real-life tournament. That Bay of Plenty team comprised Joe Tauiwi, Peter Woods and Martin Jones, all of whom would go on to play for the national sevens team; Damon Kaui, who would go on to become a Steamers centurion; Phil Werahiko, who had a great club combination with Joe Tauiwi at Ngongotaha; Kopai Erihei, who would represent New Zealand at touch rugby; Charles Bidois and Darryl Menzies, who were both yet to make their debut for the Steamers; and Paul Fairweather and Leighton Edwards. It was a team that had the perfect blend of wisdom and youth, graft and pace. It felt like a sevens team, built around players who were fit and who could make crucial decisions both in attack and defence. We would soon find out if my theory held.

Our contingent of supporters would stop over in Hong Kong to watch the Hong Kong Sevens tournament on the way to Melrose. The New Zealand team was coached by Wayne Smith that year and captained by the All Blacks and Auckland winger Terry Wright. Also in the side were four members of the North Harbour team that had conquered the National Sevens – Scott Pierce, Geoff Alley, Glen Osborne, and a particularly handy player named Eric Rush. Three of the side were Cantabrians: Paula Bale, Graeme Bachop and Dallas Seymour, and the final player was another Auckland man, Pat Lam. For many of those supporters it was a journey into the unknown – a festival of noise and colour with fast-paced and furious action on the field, and a crowd that was both intoxicating, and intoxicated. It had become clear that teams had now settled on specific plans to enable them to open up defensive screens, or control tempo, or create mismatches on quick plays. The game had evolved so much in the nine years since I had taken the sodden field in that old Government Stadium. From an abbreviated form of fifteens, it had now become its own distinct sport, complete with its own textbook plays and signature moves. New Zealand made it through to the final with high hopes of success, only to be undone by the brilliance of Fiji's Waisale Serevi and Mesake Rasari. Serevi! Now there was a name that would come to define an entire generation of sevens superstars.

———

On 11 April 1992, the first-ever Bay of Plenty side to play in the famous Melrose Sevens took the field at The Greenyards. It was a one-day knock-out tournament, which put enormous strain on the players' physical reserves. We at least had the fortune of avoiding the preliminary round, which meant a potential four games in the day rather than five, and faced the Watsonians team in our first game, or 'tie' as the matches were known in Melrose.

We had come with a plan to be aggressive in defence and it certainly worked for us. After defeating Watsonians 20–10 in our first match, we dispatched the famous Gala club in the quarterfinals with a 26–nil shutout. That result certainly set the tongues wagging in the corporate tents. Gala had played in the inaugural final in 1883 and since then had been regular winners of the event. Here they were being demolished by these Kiwi interlopers in the quarterfinals. Any hopes that Hawick – a club that had won 29 previous Melrose titles – would restore some local pride in the semifinals were dashed when we exploded out of the blocks and quickly racked up 30 points. If the tongues had been wagging before, they were damn near falling out of dropping jaws after that match.

I was a little more grounded than some of the fans. I knew from experience that each new game of sevens threw up its own distinct challenges, and in tournament play it is only the last game of the day that really matters. The final, against Kelso – a team that had won five of the last 10 titles – was going to be no walkover, of that I was certain. And so it proved, with the Bay side having to grind for every single opportunity against a Kelso team that was doing exactly the same. There was a certain beauty to it, really: aggression in the throes of exhaustion. What was even more beautiful, however, was the sound of the final whistle and the beaming smiles on my players' faces. We had won the Melrose Sevens with a 19–12 victory. It was just the second time a southern hemisphere team had ever lifted the trophy, and the first time a New Zealand team had achieved the feat. We were all nothing short of elated.

That tournament victory gave me my 'why'. Coaching gave me a purpose, a new challenge to replace the one I had missed after I'd hung up my playing boots. I knew, sitting in the changing rooms at The Greenyards after that win, as the boys contemplated how they were going to attack the giant bottle of Scotch they had just been handed at the trophy ceremony, that coaching gave me the power to pass on the knowledge I had accumulated in both sales and in rugby – that it allowed me to put into practice all of the theories

Coaching gave me a purpose, a new challenge to replace the one I had missed after I'd hung up my playing boots.

I had concocted since my first experiences of sevens back in the UK. And it gave me the chance to have an influence on success. I loved winning, always had, and this was a win to be savoured. The rest of the season, however, would be a reminder not to take anything for granted.

5

—

KNOCK, AND THE AND THE DOOR WILL OPEN

LESS THAN A month after the joy of Melrose, we launched into the fifteens season. It felt like a free fall back down to earth. We had a good side, a genuine mix of grit and intellect that I truly thought had all the requisite skills, but in some ways the harder we tried, the worse it became. I knew I was under pressure from the union to deliver results – chief among them promotion back to the first division of the National Provincial Championship – but I also wanted to rebuild the depth of Bay rugby and to bring through some of the talent I had mentored in the Colts the year before. We had some great thinkers on the game in that Bay side. Vern Cotter and Milton Haig were certainly two of them, and both would go on to enjoy successful provincial and international coaching careers of their own – Vern with Scotland and Milton with Georgia. What we perhaps lacked was a couple of players who could create something from nothing. We also lacked patience – the very thing I had evangelised to the board when I was appointed to the job.

We began the pre-season programme with a single-point loss to Hawke's Bay, followed by a loss to the touring Ireland side, another to King Country and a fourth to Western Samoa. We had two more pre-season fixtures – against North Auckland, a 16-all draw, and against Waikato when we were handsomely put away 35–11.

Before the season proper even began, my first-class record as Bay of Plenty coach read: played six, lost five, drew one. It was hardly the kind of record to inspire confidence in anyone, least of all myself. In our first competition game of the year we were beaten again, 21–19, by Taranaki. I was a new coach at this level of the game and I was the first to admit that I was struggling with the results. Again, I would lean on my business experience to look for answers to our struggles. The key thing I had learned in sales was that disappointment was an opportunity for improvement, and you could never afford to stop knocking on doors, both metaphorically and literally. I kept knocking, searching for ways to improve the team's performance, and the wins soon began to come. By the end of the regular season we had turned our pre-season disaster into a 5–3 competition record, and a date with Counties in the semifinals.

It had been a great turnaround, based on a belief in what we were trying to do, not to mention a gruelling regime of training runs designed to create a team that, collectively, would have the stamina to dig deeper than the opposition in any match we played. We won four of our last five regular-season matches that year, a feat that coincided with the introduction to top-level rugby of a 19-year-old kid called Adrian Cashmore. Adrian would later move to Auckland and the Blues where he would become a nationally prominent fullback and wing, and a two-test All Black. In those five games for me at Bay of Plenty that year he scored 62 points – a season high. In many ways, Adrian was a catalyst for many of my future selections. He was the epitome of the adage, 'If you're good enough, you're old enough.'

As a team, we weren't good enough to defeat Counties that year, and my first season in charge finished with an agonising two-point loss in Pukekohe. While naturally disappointed that we didn't have enough that year to make it back to the first division, I still felt the trajectory over the last month of competition had been positive. When I was told that the coach's job would be advertised at the end of the season, I was confident that I would be reappointed, having made the case before that the quest for a return to the top league would be one that took some time. The board did not agree. Bruce Cameron, my former Bay of Plenty team-mate, called me with the news. 'Sorry Titch,' he said. 'We've decided to go another way.' Matt Te Pou was handed the job for the next season. I was out the door.

It was another agonising time. I was naturally competitive and wanted desperately to be given another chance to build on the work I had put in during that 1992 season. Coaching was in some ways less a calling than an addiction. I loved the rush of watching a plan come together and the thrill of seeing a player repay selection with a great performance. It never felt like a part-time hobby for me. I had attacked it as if it was a co-job, one that neatly complemented my role with Bay Engineers. I didn't just *want* to coach, I *needed* to coach. Despite the disappointment of being replaced in the top job, I decided that I would return to the Colts. Hell, I was a Bay man, loyal to the core. If I couldn't be in charge of the top team, I could at least help produce the next generation that would play for it. It was another door to knock on.

Coaching allows you to constantly think in terms of performance. Sometimes, in business and in life, we forget that our deeds and our results become our most effective marketing tool. Anyone can be successful in sales in the short term. You can win a big account with a hint of chutzpah and a whiff of charm, but if you don't enhance your reputation every day, by looking to improve your service or your offering, there will come a time when you start to miss opportunities. When you dedicate yourself to knocking on doors – to searching for opportunities – what you will find is that people begin to knock on yours. In 1993, and quite out of the blue, a remarkable opportunity came my way.

Having been relieved of duties as head coach of Bay of Plenty, I thought back to the start of the season and the remarkable experience we all had enjoyed in Melrose. I enjoyed the tactical challenge of fifteens, but I had genuinely relished the family-like atmosphere within the smaller, closer sevens set-up. In 1993, the Sevens Rugby World Cup would be held in Scotland and the coaching job had been advertised by the NZRFU. Never one to be twice shy, I applied for the role, and was duly interviewed in Wellington. For the second time in a matter of months, I was to be unsuccessful. Peter Thorburn was selected for the job, and I was once again in a coaching limbo. But a few weeks later I received a phone call. Would I be interested in taking the New Zealand Sevens B team to a tournament in Fiji in the lead-up to the Hong Kong Sevens? I had no idea New Zealand even had a B team, and even less of an idea about what to expect in a Fijian tournament, but how could I say no? Somewhat bemused, but still thrilled to receive the call, I accepted the role. The next thing I knew, I was handed a team and we were landing in Nadi. What was to unfold over the following week would stay with me for a lifetime.

I knew Fiji loved sevens rugby. I had seen their national side in action in Hong Kong and marvelled at their ability to win tournaments with a brand of rugby that was part brutal, part beautiful, and wholly magical. They were gifted athletes – supremely agile and mostly incredibly fast. Their affinity for support play and sixth sense for exposing any half-chance had long made them fan favourites in Hong Kong. I knew all of that, but for the first time in my life I had arrived in the factory, so to speak, the island laboratory that every year produced players imbued with the winning formula.

The narrow and enchanting Queens Road from Nadi in the west to Suva in the south charts a serpentine course through cane farms and collections of corrugated-iron shopfronts and workshops, forested hills and farmland, before hugging the windswept coral coast from Cuvu Beach to Somosomo Bay, passing through the river-mouth citadel of Sigatoka with its proud roundabout sign proclaiming it to be 'Rugby Town'. It is a big boast in a country in which rugby-ness is next to godliness, but it is home to the famous Nadroga side – synonymous with sevens and with success. The trip takes a good three hours, depending on traffic and stray livestock. It is an unhurried journey – the national speed limit is 80 kilometres per hour but all traffic slows through each of the many small villages along the way – and one during which you cannot fail to fall for the charm of the people and the place. It is a procession of roadside stalls and cooking fires, broad and welcoming smiles, and people on the move, walking to or from one place or another with a purpose that remains a mystery to the casual observer.

Many a tourist has been lured by the resort walls, festooned in the pinks and purples of bougainvillea blooms, or the stretches of white-sand beaches along which tower swaying palm trees, but I was taken by another scene altogether. Everywhere I looked, in every village, on every patch of grass or bare clay, there was a game of rugby under way. It didn't matter if it was one-on-one or thirty-on-thirty, it seemed whenever I glanced out the minivan window I saw a game in progress, and heard kids shouting and laughing. It was the sound of Fijian rugby; it was the sight of the soul of sevens.

It was this: pure, unadulterated joy.

What an eye-opener it was. It was one thing to want a team to have fun, it was quite another to witness boys and men belting ten layers of hell out of one another and genuinely enjoying it. I realised that this was Fiji's great weapon: rugby was a game to be enjoyed at all costs, and winning was the reward for relishing the challenge. From that point on, I understood why they were so good. Rugby was a proving ground as much as a playground. Sevens, with its premium on pace and strength, footwork and flair, was the sport that encapsulated the energy of those islands.

We were no match for the locals at that tournament. In fact, we were no match for the Canadian side either who, along with the Suva team, put us to the sword in pool play. Out of cup contention, we at least made it through to the plate final, but we were handed another harsh lesson by Australia. The tournament lasted for three days, played in energy-sapping heat at Suva's National Stadium. By day three we were exhausted. Sitting back, we watched the cup final as Fiji played Suva in front of an absolutely raucous crowd. It was a dazzling game of sevens, played at such a pace we were left to wonder how both sides could still look so unfatigued.

Fiji would win their home tournament and the following week would make their fourth consecutive Hong Kong final. They would be upset in that match by Western Samoa, ending a run of three straight tournament victories. It was a loss that shocked the Fijian fans and, having returned to New Zealand with a newfound respect for their love, passion and affinity for the game, I understood why. I also knew this: it was time that New Zealand treated sevens with the respect it deserved. If an island nation with less than a quarter of our population could become the dominant force in the game, surely we had the resources and the talent to take them on.

To me it was simple: sevens needed to be treated as its own distinct game and I could make sure it was given that kind of attention.

Something needed to change in the way we looked at the game. In Hong Kong that year the New Zealand side had been defeated by the eventual champions, Western Samoa, in the semifinals. A couple of weeks later, at the Sevens World Cup, the New Zealand team was knocked out at the quarterfinals stage.

Peter Thorburn stood down from the coaching role following the World Cup disappointment and I had a decision to make. Did I really want to put myself forward again if there was a chance I would once more be passed over for the job? The short answer was yes. After Fiji, I knew this was the game for me. I still wanted to coach fifteens, but I understood how I could have an impact on the sevens programme, how I could unleash the talent we had in New Zealand. I thought about all I had learned over the years that I had played, researched and coached the game. I thought, too, about how I had always gone after opportunities when they presented themselves. It was time to lay it on the line.

I once again flew to Wellington to be interviewed for the role, this time with a very clear idea of how I wanted to pitch myself to the appointment panel. To me it was simple: sevens needed to be treated as its own distinct game and I could make sure it was given that kind of attention. I wanted to unearth and to nurture a team of players who were specialists in a sport that for too long had been treated simply as rugby without props. It was so much more than that, so much more nuanced and complex. I knew that I had the background and the knowledge to do the job, that I could identify the right players and get them in the right shape for the sport. All I needed was the chance to prove it.

I thought I had made a compelling argument, and it seems the board agreed. A few days later, I received a call: I was now the coach of the New Zealand Sevens team. There had been some luck along the way, but to me it proved the value of knocking on the door. If I had packed up my toys and stormed out of the sandpit after my demotion at Bay of Plenty, I would never have applied for the job in 1993. If I hadn't applied then, I would never have been given the chance to take the New Zealand B side to Fiji. If I hadn't been to Fiji, I may never have truly grasped the real essence of the game and how the right attitude on the right kind of athlete could be such a wonderful recipe for success.

─────────

It was time to find those players, and that required plenty of travel. I was again indebted to Warwick Talbut, who did not hesitate in giving me his blessing to pursue the job. As always, he was a man who lived what he preached and he never wanted to get in the way of the passions of his people. He could tell that this was a watershed moment for me. Lord knows he had spent many an hour listening to my theories on the game, and many a longer hour providing invaluable mentoring over the last couple of years when I had missed out on coaching positions or was struggling to find the formula to get teams into a winning groove. I was also indebted to my family – we had welcomed into the world a second child, Kylie, a couple of years earlier, and I knew the extra workload had an impact on family life.

Knowing that the people closest to me supported me in my quest, I vowed to do everything I could to make the venture a successful one. As soon as I could, I began scouting for players. No tournament was too small, and no player irrelevant. If I wanted to find players who fit the bill, I would search for them anywhere I could. I spent that summer at club events, and the provincial qualifying series, marking names in my notebook, and discussing various players with local coaches and personalities. In March 1994, the local sevens season culminated with the National Rugby Sevens Tournament in Palmerston North. It was the last chance for players to impress, and I wasn't the only one casting an eye over the talent on show. Joining me that weekend in Palmerston North were the All Blacks selection panel of Laurie Mains, Ross Cooper and Earle Kirton. It was in many ways an unlikely trio – Laurie, the stern southerner who had been All Blacks coach since the 1992 season, was a hard man with firm opinions; Ross, who was the current Counties coach, had a laconic manner and a moustache of epic proportions; and Earle, the Wellington dentist with a penchant for scarves, had a certain appreciation of flamboyance. The three men were there to help me select the team. It is fair to say that our thoughts on the matter were somewhat disparate in nature.

Throughout the weekend, I would meet with the others periodically to discuss certain players, but I remained largely on my own as I watched the games unfold. It was a policy I had adopted when I first got the job – to sit and follow players I wanted to follow without the distraction of conversation or the threat of having my thinking clouded by other people's opinions. The time for that discussion was after the action, when notes and thoughts could be compared in a setting away from the games. I could tell from the conversations we had during those two days that we – the selectors and I – were looking at things very differently. In essence, we had a massive disconnect between what we saw as the crucial attributes required to play the game. It felt as if the others found it hard to separate the two distinct versions of rugby – sevens and fifteens – and as such they placed a premium on one set of skills and I on another. We were at loggerheads for much of the weekend, and at times discussions boiled over into flat-out arguments. In my mind, I had the right as convener of the panel to hold sway over the final decision (remembering my thoughts on committees and cul-de-sacs), and I had done the legwork around the country to ensure I got to see the players in as many different situations as possible. In other words, I felt that my background in the game and my research on the talent on show gave me a right to select the players I wanted.

Call it stubbornness, call it pig-headedness, call it what you will. I was damned if I was going to get the job of coaching a team only to find that team was one I did not pick. As much as I respected those men, and I still do, I had to take a drastic step. After another argument about when we should actually name the team – Laurie and the others wanted to name it before the final, which was anathema to me – I went with my gut instinct. I wrote my own team list, wandered over to the NZRFU chairman, and handed him the piece of paper. It was not the team that had been agreed to by the others, but it was the team I wanted. When the team was eventually read out, Laurie was apoplectic. I suspect it was the first time in a long while that anyone had actually had the temerity to question him, let alone so brazenly go behind his back. He tracked me down and told me in no uncertain terms that he would not ever waste his time helping me out again. The others were not as put out, but by the same token they were hardly impressed. I am not sure what the chairman thought of it all, but he duly named the team, and that was that.

After the final, which Counties won convincingly over Waikato with the assistance of an 18-year-old Wesley College kid by the name of Jonah Tali Lomu, coach and team gathered in the changing rooms at the Palmerston North Showgrounds for our first-ever meeting. In the room that day were some men who would become synonymous with New Zealand sevens, and some who would go on to achieve worldwide superstardom. I could tell it was a squad capable of working extremely hard. That was what I had been looking for on the club fields and during the domestic tournaments. As I shook each of their hands and discussed their selection, I felt the anticipation building. These were *my* guys. Maybe there was a lesson in all of it. If the door won't open no matter how hard you knock, sometimes you just need to find another door. In extreme cases, there is one other option: just make one of your own.

PART TWO

—

UNLEASHING A LEGACY

6

SOLID
FOUNDATIONS

EVERYTHING I HAD learned so far in my life was about to be poured into coaching the New Zealand Sevens team. It couldn't just be about the game. If I wanted this team to succeed, it had to be a team that shared common values and one that took a holistic approach to winning. I thought long and hard about how I wanted to transfer that information to the players, and how I wanted them to respond. Digging deep, I retreated all the way back to childhood to peel back the layers of my experience, and what it had taught me.

I thought about humility and how we had been brought up in that tiny railway house in Rotorua. We weren't a family of great financial means and what we did have we appreciated. The two most important words in our house were 'please' and 'thank you'. Those dual notions of respect and gratitude had to underpin everything we did as a team – in training, in camp, and on the field. When you learn to treasure the opportunities you are given, you learn how to make the most of each and every one of them.

I thought, too, about hard work, and the long shifts my father put in on the railways. He always did what needed to be done – no short cuts, no half measures. That's where his personal pride was derived from, and it was that work ethic that he had passed on to each of his children. We were expected to pull our weight around the house and we did so because we knew it was important to contribute. We could not be a team that thought anything great would be easily won. We all had a job to do and we would do it right.

There were business lessons, too. An imperative to build a solid reputation by earning and showing respect. We had to set our goals and then deliver on our ambition by doing the things we said we would do. In that way, we had the chance to catapult the game of sevens into the national sporting consciousness. It was still a game that went largely unnoticed in the reportage of rugby in New Zealand. We could be the team to change that. We could be the ones to put sevens on the map.

As I honed my thinking around the team, I was also aware of that thrill of the chase – that hunger to go after an account or a client, to follow a playing or coaching dream. It was a hunger I had always tried to nourish, and I wanted to make sure everyone in the side was just as motivated by their own desires to be the best they could be. If I could cultivate those things: humility, gratitude, hunger and hard work, the rest would take care of itself.

For my part, it was up to me to learn everything I could about the game, and the players I had. Just as I had craved knowledge as a young trainee with International Harvester, I would devour anything I could find on sevens strategy and training. That would be the way I would earn the respect of the players; it would be knowledge that led to trust, and trust that allowed me to have a leadership relationship with the men in my side. First, though, I was going to make them hurt.

Sevens was still a game that went largely unnoticed in the reportage of rugby in New Zealand. We could be the team to change that. We could be the ones to put sevens on the map.

As was the habit of New Zealand teams of the time, our first training base was at Onewa Domain on the North Shore of Auckland, across the road from the union's hotel of choice, the Poenamo. On the Monday following the National Sevens championships in Palmerston North we assembled as a team there and prepared for our first training run together. I needed to make sure the players I'd picked were ready for what was going to be the toughest session they had ever undertaken. Knowing I was likely to leave a few of the lads in shock, I had one job to do first: find the foundations upon which all else could be built.

When coaches talk about the foundations of the team, they surely speak of their most trusted players. If you are going to stand in front of a group and give orders that group are not going to like, you need your captain and your lieutenant. It was patently clear that I had two men who would be those guys for me. One was a wiry bloke with quick feet and a quicker wit who was born and raised in the Far North, and the other was a tough and physically imposing Cantabrian with a clenched-jaw determination to put himself through ten levels of hell on the field. They would be the guys I had to get on board. Undoubtedly, the foundations of that team were Eric Rush and Dallas Seymour.

Eric and Dallas were the high-profile sevens men of the time. They were both supremely humble, hard-working, very good at what they did in the game, and truly professional. In many ways, they were the prototype players for the Super Rugby age, which was still a couple of years away from coming to fruition. I sought their counsel early with the aim of building a professional and personal relationship with them – professional because they needed to know that I had a job as coach to get the very best out of the team and I would therefore have to make some big decisions that weren't always going to be popular; and personal because I needed to get along with them in order to achieve their total buy-in.

Both men commanded an enormous amount of respect within the team, and I wanted to earn their respect as well. If I could do that, then they would be able to be my go-betweens and tone-setters. They would be the ones to lead that programme together because I knew they would always empty the tank for me in training and any time they wore the black jersey. Dallas was nicknamed 'Nails' for a reason: he was that bloody tough. Eric, well, he was inarguably the greatest sevens captain New Zealand has ever produced. There was another reason those two men were crucial to the team. They had both been in the New Zealand Sevens team for a number of years and I knew they were craving some overdue success. In fact, Eric and Dallas had first played for the New Zealand team in Hong Kong in 1988, and in the six years they had been a part of that tournament they had reached five finals and lifted the trophy just once, in 1989. Three of the finals losses had been against Fiji, and one, their first, had come against Australia. If there were two men who were more motivated for success than them, then I surely had not met them.

I wanted to share with Eric and Dallas what I had told the NZRFU during my interview for the job. I needed them to know that I believed sevens was its own sport and that the reason I thought the team had failed to live up to expectations at the Sevens World Cup the year before, and for a number of years in Hong Kong, was because the team selection did not reflect the specialist skills required in the game. It was my intention, I confided in them, to make sure from here on in that we had a squad that was 100 per cent sevens focused. To do that, we were going to have to train harder than ever before.

Encouragingly, not once did I detect an ounce of trepidation on their part. Whether they thought I was bluffing or not, I could not tell, but with each nod of agreement I was becoming more and more emboldened to set this ship on the course I had plotted. In my heart, I knew that whatever I threw at the squad in that first session would not be enough to break either man, and if it broke anyone else, they would be there to pick up the pieces. That was the foundation of my team: two intensely proud veterans who knew what it was going to take to win. I was so fortunate to have them in my side.

They, however, probably weren't feeling so fortunate to have me as a coach – at least not after the first morning in camp. I needed to test everyone in the squad so we had a baseline to work from, and I had not forgotten my days in training with Ron Mahy, the tennis guru. Just as he would leave the racquets in the bag for entire sessions, there was not a ball in sight when the players wandered across to the fields for that first hit-out as a team. I had devised a testing plan that would take the boys to the limits and, hopefully, beyond. It started with sprints and ended with death.

———

If there was one paramount element of sevens play, it was support. A rugby field can feel like a vast wilderness when eight people are removed from each side. Whether on attack or in defence, the game is about manipulating space to create mismatches. The way to do this is to make sure you have someone on hand to assist at all times. That means each player has to be able to cover an enormous amount of ground, and do so over and over again. I wanted to develop a training programme that put a premium on support play and finally, after putting that first squad through speed and fitness testing, I threw them the ball and said let's play.

The game I set for them was a simulation of sevens – not full contact or tackle – with a premium placed on support. The idea was to see how hard the guys could work to get themselves into a support position. If a player was scragged by his opponent and a team-mate hadn't arrived in time to help, then the ball was turned over and the other team had the chance to attack. It was halfway between touch and tackle but with one key difference: there were no breaks. It was my first chance to set the standard for the team and I didn't want to let that chance slide. I had my theories on how the game should be played, and by whom, and I needed to be sure that those theories could have practical application.

We played seven minutes at full pace, and then another seven, and then another. I loved what I saw, not because of some masochistic fetish for inflicting pain, but because I could tell the players were feeling the strain and were playing on regardless. It was a brutal session, one which would be repeated innumerable times over the course of my coaching career, and it told me all I needed to know about the mental and physical strength of the players. In the back of my mind was a conversation I'd had with Eric before training began. I had asked him how hard Peter Thorburn, the previous coach, had trained them. Eric, no doubt sensing a trap, hesitated briefly before telling me he had trained them pretty hard. I watched them running, saw the pain etched on their faces, and thought, well, 'Not this hard.'

Having had my fill, I finally blew the whistle. Players dropped to the Onewa Domain turf, spent and relieved that for now the pain was over. Once he had caught his breath, Eric called out, 'Hey Titch, what do you call that game?'

'I don't know,' I responded. It was an honest response, too. I hadn't even thought of a name for it.

'Well, we'll just call it death,' he said.

And death it became.

I think now of the genius of Eric's quip. It was both a way to poke fun at the pain the guys had just been through, and a signal to me that no matter what I threw at this team, they would come through the other side. Among his many fantastic qualities, Eric had a knack for delivering positive messages in very subtle ways. By naming that game 'death' he was challenging the team to flip the pain on its head. After all, if they could cheat death, then imagine what else they could achieve. That notion of positive messaging resonated deeply with me. I had resolved to make sure that as a coach I would always seek to be positive in my communication with the team. I wouldn't always achieve that, but it was well worth trying. It was another valuable lesson I had been taught by Warwick Talbut in business. He had always found a way, even in the most challenging circumstances, to accentuate the positive. If we had lost a pitch, or a client spend had dropped, we would have a courageous conversation about why it may have happened, and quickly move on to how we could get better next time. You can't wallow in disappointment if you are motivated to walk on water.

There is no doubt that first training day with the New Zealand Sevens squad set a tone for what was to come, and I was enormously grateful that I had leaders – *foundations* – like Eric and Dallas in that side. It would have been so easy for them to turn that team against the new guy after that day. Remember, those two men had already spent six years in the black jersey before my arrival on the scene. They had more experience in the game than the bloke coaching them, and here he was driving them into the ground at the very first opportunity. That they backed me from the very start was the key to everything. That they always maintained a sense of humour helped, too.

I could sense as the days in camp unfolded that this team was fast developing a sense of unity under the pressure of training. The harder I pushed, the harder the players pushed each other. It was a 'no man left behind' mentality, a galvanising force that forged a deep and meaningful connection between the players in a short space of time. If they were going to be suffering in training, they were going to suffer as one. Unity is what makes a family tick, and a sevens team is a family team. Eric and Dallas led that metamorphosis, and everyone else followed their lead. At the end of the week, I knew this team was ready to play. We boarded a plane and headed to Fiji for the international tournament. If we were going to be competitive in Hong Kong in 1994, we needed to test ourselves against the best first.

It was good to be able to unleash the squad in Fiji. They had worked extremely hard during that first week in camp, and I could tell they just wanted to get on the field and get amongst it. We had drawn Malaysia, Tonga and Vanuatu in our pool and I felt a little sorry for them as the boys ripped into their work, racking up more than 100 points over the three matches to set up a quarterfinal showdown with Western Samoa. Again, our opponents were blown away as the boys racked up another 38 points and conceded just one try. We were in a good space – playing with gusto and width. Everything we had worked on during the week was being put into practice and we were confident heading into the semifinal against Eastern Fiji.

That would be as far as confidence would take us. Pushing all the way to extra time, the team was finally defeated 21–14. Eastern Fiji would go on to defeat their national side on the way to the tournament triumph, which was some consolation, but we were disappointed with the early exit. If there was a positive in the loss, it was that we had played some of the wider squad players throughout the tournament. That had given everyone a chance to prove their value for Hong Kong and it had given me the opportunity to think hard about what, and who, it was going to take to win the big tournament.

Returning to New Zealand, we redoubled our efforts in training with an even greater understanding of what was required to succeed as a team. The extra-time defeat in Fiji was used as motivation. If we had been a little bit fitter, would we have been able to make better decisions? What if we were in that position in Hong Kong? How would we handle it better the next time? We now had the perfect pretext for putting in the extra yards and, with a few more days in camp, we felt ready to head to the big show, safe in the knowledge that if we were going to lose, it was not going to be through lack of preparation.

I may have felt prepared for the games, but I was not prepared for what the Hong Kong event had grown into. In 1983, I had played for New Zealand in the old Government Stadium in front of a few thousand fans. In 1994, it seemed the entire city was thronged with sevens revellers from around the world, all preparing to descend on the new Hong Kong Stadium in Wan Chai. The new stadium – sans seats – had hosted the sevens for the first time the year before, and had only just been completed in time for this year's event. It was a wonderful stadium, with its massive arched roofing over the grandstands, and its open ends backdropped by the scale of the city outside. There was just a special vibe about the Hong Kong tournament. It was the sevens equivalent of Mecca. Although Melrose can always lay claim to being the birthplace of the game, Hong Kong is where sevens drank its yard glass. In all the times that I would visit that event, it never once lost its charm. If anything, it seemed to get better with every passing year.

In 1994, Eric and Dallas seemed to have the city on lockdown. There wasn't a place we would go as a team without them being instantly recognised by sevens fans from around the world. It was remarkable to see the esteem in which they were held by supporters, and it gave the team a real sense of pride to know that those two men had already made their mark on this tournament. I could sense that the others, having witnessed the adulation first-hand, wanted to make their own mark over the weekend, which gave me enormous encouragement as a coach. I had no issue at all with eight guys wishing to emulate my two leaders. In fact, it was exactly what I needed them to do.

The two things about that team that gave me the most pleasure were that they all just wanted to be there and they were a very close-knit bunch of guys. I had made some big calls on selections, going against the thoughts of the All Blacks panel at the time I picked the squad, but seeing them together in Hong Kong, and feeling their desire to go out and give it everything they had to give, I knew I had been right to trust my instinct. There was still a

Although Melrose can always lay claim to being the birthplace of the game, Hong Kong is where sevens drank its yard glass.

lot of pressure on me – the proof of the pudding would be in the eating – but in terms of personnel and preparation, we couldn't have been better served.

In that first side in Hong Kong were the veterans, Rush and Seymour; my Bay of Plenty trio of Peter Woods, Joe Tauiwi and Martin Jones; All Blacks halfback Graeme Bachop; Hawke's Bay's leading try-scorer Aaron Hamilton; the powerful Counties ball runner Luke Erenavula; and the two youngest players in the team, a hard-case fullback by the name of Glen Osborne and teenage sensation-in-waiting Jonah Lomu. I had a preferred starting seven that I had decided on through watching training and the tournament play in Fiji, and I felt it was a team that walked the line between valuable experience and youthful energy.

We opened that tournament with a big victory over Malaysia, and followed it up with another pool-stage win over Tonga. I could tell that the guys were in great shape, and so could everyone else watching. We were not going to get carried away, however. As we had learned in Fiji a few weeks earlier, tournament sevens is always about the next game. Things can change very quickly if you take your foot off the throat. Our quarterfinal, against France, was much tougher than the previous two games, and a good lesson for us in avoiding complacency. We got through the match with a 21–12 victory but, more importantly, we knew that any slip-up could be costly. Especially in a semifinal, which we would now have to play against Fiji.

There is always an element of the unknown when you take on Fiji. On my visits to Suva I had been absolutely blown away both by the passion and the talent for the game there. It was as if Fijian players all had the ability to conjure something from nothing, and in Hong Kong they had perhaps the most remarkable sevens wizard of all time, Waisale Serevi, the star attraction since his debut there in 1989. The fans loved him, and it was easy to see why. His game sense was second to none, and he could have opposition teams scrambling with subtle shifts in direction or a burst of blistering acceleration. As clever as he was elusive, he was the master of his team's destiny. He was their diminutive commander-in-chief.

I knew we had to target him. If we could take away Serevi's space and time, if we could make sure he was not the one dictating terms to us, then we could go a long way to shutting down the Fijian threat. Sevens is a different game to fifteens, certainly, but they both revolve around genuine playmakers. If you shut down the playmaker, you pressurise a team into making bad decisions. There are two ways to do that – harassing them when they have the ball, and making sure you are running at them when they don't. We had a guy who could run with the ball, and he was about to pick out the perfect guy to run at.

There are defining moments you remember as a coach, no matter how long you have been in the job, and the moment that big kid from Counties, Jonah Lomu, grabbed the ball and ran around, then over, and finally through the great Fijian, I knew we were going to get the job done. It was as if in that one play, Jonah had crushed the will of the opposition and simultaneously provided all the fuel our fire needed. We would finish with a 28–14 victory, and set up a final showdown with Australia, a team that was stacked with some of the best rugby players that nation had ever produced. We all knew the names – Gregan, Little, Horan, Wilson and Campese among them – but I was sure that if they hadn't heard the name

Jonah Lomu before the game, they certainly had afterwards. Led by Eric Rush with sensational support from the rest of his team, the Kiwis finally got the win in Hong Kong, defeating Australia 32–20 in a try-fest. For Eric and Dallas, it was a special moment to be holding that trophy again. For the others, it was a victory to savour. For Glen Osborne, it was doubly sweet. He was awarded the trophy for best and fairest player of the tournament, something he would boast about for the next 24 . . . years.

I stood there on the field afterwards and savoured every second. The crowd had invaded the pitch after the match and the players were mobbed by supporters, all keen to capture an autograph or just a moment with the stars. I looked up to the South Stand, which fans had already decided was to be party central of the tournament. It was a sea of colour and carnage in the gloaming. My players were beaming smiles of genuine satisfaction. The fun could begin now that the hard work was done. As for Jonah, he had taken his first giant steps to becoming the most recognisable rugby player in the world. David Campese and Waisale Serevi certainly knew he was on his way to very big things. They still have his footprints on their chests to prove it.

7

SMALL THINGS, BIG DIFFERENCE

WHEN I HAD first coached Bay of Plenty in 1992, I had put myself forward as a New Zealand resource coach, and I had also signed myself up for as many training courses as I could find. I was looking for ways to become better as a trainer of players, and for methods that may help my teams get an edge – no matter how small – on their opponents. I had come to understand that nutrition was a massive factor in performance and I enlisted the help of nutritionist Jeni Pearce to help me better understand how my players could benefit from a change in diet.

It would become the thing my players most often talked about, after the rigours of trainings. Eric Rush would have you believe that I once caught the team feasting on McDonald's at Auckland Airport and went through the roof. To this day, he thinks that I'm the only man who could have passed through airport security and been able to come back through again on the suspicion one of my players was eating a Big Mac. As with all tales of rugby, there has been a great deal of exaggeration over the years, but the truth is, I didn't want my players to be eating crappy food. In fact, I expressly banned it.

It may seem archaic that I would tell grown men not to eat a burger or an ice cream, but it was part and parcel of what we had to do in the high-performance environment. I knew guys like Eric had a sweet tooth, but having a policy around certain foods wasn't necessarily for their benefit. It was a message to everyone in the team that one rule applied to all – even the captain, a man with seven years of international experience. In fairness, Eric did put a lot of effort into that side of his training. He, like so many of the boys who came into the team, didn't have a great diet when I first joined the side. I spent many meetings with him convincing him to change his eating habits, hoping that he would see the light. I knew that he would have many more years of success if he treated food the same way he treated every other part of his training regime. He knew it, too, even if he didn't like the sound of it. It was important to me that he be the one to lead the nutrition side of the team. The message was simple: if Eric could make those changes in his life, everyone else in the team could as well.

What's good for one is good for all. That was Eric's theory on the team, and that's why we instituted a blanket policy around what the team ate. There were players in those teams that could have devoured a bucket of chicken and probably still put in a match-winning performance, such was their natural ability. But there were others for whom diet was a constant challenge. You have to make a decision as a coach: Am I going to reward a chosen few, or am I going to drive everyone to reach their level? The answer was very clear to me, and out the door went fried foods and fizzy drinks. That also went for the management team, such as it was in the early years. It was no problem for me as I had already been converted to clean eating, but we all had to abide by the same set of rules whether we were playing or coaching.

There was also one other thing: no alcohol was allowed in camp or during tournaments. That certainly had caused some consternation in Hong Kong in 1994 – the boys were accustomed to having a few beers in the week leading into the tournament – but it was a bottom line for me. I am quite happy to savour a glass of wine or a beer with family and friends, but alcohol has no place in an athlete's bloodstream, and had no place for me while I was with the team.

———

As a coach, setting expectations is absolutely vital. If you don't, how can you expect players to follow you? Your team needs to know exactly what you want from them. In that way, they can easily assess where they stand, and will not be surprised if they don't pass muster. In coaching, just as in business, too often players and staff are allowed to drift, not knowing what the benchmark is and therefore failing to reach it. If you cannot tell someone what their role is, how are you going to help them fulfil it, and then guide them back onto the path when they stray from it? How can you expect them to deliver results? After 1994, my guys knew exactly what was required of them in training and in performance: nutrition was the guide to keep them on the straight and narrow.

It wasn't simply about setting rules, it was about educating the guys to make the right choices. As more and more young players came into the selection frame, I also took the chance to impress upon families that their own decisions and lifestyle choices were going to have an impact on their kids' chances of making it in sevens. There's no point bringing a player into camp, teaching him to eat well and train hard, if at the end of each camp the same player heads back home where there are no healthy eating options or a lack of support for their endeavours. We need buy-in not just from the player, but from the player's entire family and friends network. Players are the result of the people they are made from, and the people they hang out with. Seen in this light, the nutrition element of our environment was simply part of a holistic approach to wellbeing.

There would be plenty of grumbling along the way (mainly of the tummy variety), but in my eyes it was abundantly clear that high fats and sugars were not the recipe for success. Neither was red meat – something I forbid the players from eating at least two days out from each tournament. Yes, there were times when the players thought it was all a little over the top, especially when I would bring up the subject of what they had for breakfast after a sluggish training run or an indifferent performance. However, the signal to them was clear: we were going to be the most disciplined team in world sevens, and if we were, we would also be the best. In this context, Jeni's advice on nutrition was invaluable. Our style of training also required plenty of calories, and she was always on hand to design the appropriate eating plans for the team. It was never about starving them, although the late Norm Berryman may have had a dissenting opinion. I well remember his first experience in camp. He couldn't get through one of the training sessions and had to pull out, taking a seat on the sideline as the rest of the team completed a number of sprints. I said to him that I was actually impressed that he hadn't thrown up. He shot me a withering look and said matter-of-factly, 'I would have if you let us eat anything.' I was in stitches about that for days.

The nutrition quandary became a matter of trust. If I could get the guys to see how much a healthy diet aided in their training and performance, I could help them create lifelong habits – for themselves and, with any luck, those around them. That meant they would be better prepared next time they came into camp, and we could make incremental improvements rather than having to go back to step one and start again. I knew the guys saw the benefit, and the fact that it became a running joke in the team was just their way of dealing with the fact they were going without their favourite treats. Besides, I have never known a chocolate that tastes better than a gold medal feels around your neck.

———

Success breeds trust, and in 1994 we had been successful in Hong Kong. The benefit was that I was able to retain a core of experience and augment that with new talent coming through. That core, if your culture is right, will pass on the knowledge and set the expectations for the new players, and they in turn will grow and do same for the players following them. That succession is a weapon in sport – it's an area in which the All Blacks have excelled over a long period of time – and there have been stages in my career when we had that balance just right. The first three years of my tenure certainly stand out in that regard.

I was finding a different kind of balance. In 1995, I was asked to reapply for the Bay of Plenty coaching job after the team had spent a further two years in second division. Sevens was still four years away from getting a full world series, which meant Hong Kong remained the one key fixture, in New Zealand rugby's eyes at least, every year. I felt I had unfinished business with the Bay side, and was reappointed head coach for the upcoming season. I was blessed that I could still retain my role with Bay Engineers and took the job with the full blessing of Warwick Talbut and the company. It gave me a new drive for efficiency and time management, but also

If your culture is right, that core of experience will pass on the knowledge and set the expectations for the new players, and they in turn will grow and do the same for the players following them.

allowed me to develop as a rugby coach. Once more, I stressed to the board that getting back to the first division was going to be a five-year proposition. I knew I had told them that once before, but this time I was adamant. If they wanted a sustainable, successful team, they would have to allow it to develop over time. I was happy to oversee that development, but I needed their support. Just as I was clear with my players about expectations, I had to be clear with my prospective employers as well. Again, that clarity of thought is crucial in any part of life: Say what you want, and do what you say, and the rest will take care of itself.

For now, I had to take care of finding a new team of players. I knew that the core of the team would be in place, pending their form at the national tournament. Eric Rush, Dallas Seymour, Peter Woods, Joe Tauiwi and Jonah Lomu were all starting players in 1994 and I would once again need their leadership and drive for the upcoming season. In those early days, I could select up to 40 players in my initial training squad of the national team – something I would look back on in future years and pine for – and there was no shortage of talent on display at that year's National Rugby Sevens Tournament. Interestingly, after I had impressed upon the guys the year before that we had a chance in Hong Kong to put sevens on the map, the 1995 *New Zealand Rugby Almanack* had taken notice. For the first time ever, the official record of everything rugby in this country had a section dedicated to the National Sevens, including every result from the tournament and a list of past champions. It may seem trifling to many, but the acknowledgement certainly meant something to the players and those of us who were passionate about the sport.

Jonah, of course, had become a household name thanks to his debut for the All Blacks in the 1994 season. He was the youngest debutant in the history of the national team, but did not enjoy the best of starts, playing in a losing test series against a visiting French side that exposed some of the weaker elements in his game, not to mention his inexperience. Still, he was going to be a star, that much we could all see, and in sevens there was no better sight than him running rings around the opposition. He was joined at the 1995 national championships by a Fijian flyer called Joeli Vidiri who could absolutely terrorise opposition teams, and the two of them together in one side was a sight to behold. Their presence at the nationals did plenty to attract attention, both from opponents and from the press, with their eye-catching and ultimately title-winning play. I, on the other hand, had spotted someone half the size but no less gifted. He was a skinny kid with a shaved head, playing for Manawatu. I watched him track back on defence and drag Wellington's Filo Tiatia to the ground, which was akin to watching David topple Goliath, and then I saw him run with such grace and speed that I damn near had to pinch myself. His name was Christian Cullen. And I needed him in sevens.

It felt good to be back into training, and I could immediately sense that all the groundwork of the year before was going to pay off. There's no doubt that awareness of the training had already spread through the rugby community and it was common knowledge that if you were picked in my training camps and sevens squads you were going to get smashed. That gave us a sense of purpose, a sort of strange sadomasochistic bragging right with players who genuinely seemed in awe as the word travelled throughout the country. Over time, the Super Rugby pre-season programmes

It was common knowledge that if you were picked in my training camps and sevens squads you were going to get smashed.

would certainly become increasingly demanding as the concepts of sports science and strength and conditioning were embedded in the professional game but, in the early days of the New Zealand Sevens side, our boys helped create the legend that continues to this day. A big part of the unity within the team stemmed from the fact they had a shared experience of suffering. And they wore it like a badge of honour.

Jonah returned to camp in 1995 and looked genuinely pleased to be back in the environment. The previous year had been tough on him as he was exposed to the glare of the public spotlight and the harsh realities of All Blacks rugby. He was comfortable in the sevens programme, and was encouraged endlessly by Eric and others, all of whom looked at Jonah like he was the big little brother. It wasn't just talk either. Every time Jonah would pull out of a set of shuttles or need to take a break from a sprint session, someone would come and grab him, force him back to his feet and get in and finish it with him. As a coach, I was just so pleased when I saw things like that. It was the embodiment of team spirit. It was what a family would do.

We duly got through the training week and once again jetted off to Fiji for the Suva tournament. Earlier in the year, I had taken a team to Punta del Este in Uruguay and Mar del Plata in Argentina for two tournaments designed to give me the chance to blood some younger players and to give them valuable game time. We had been knocked out in the quarterfinals in Uruguay but defeated Fiji in the final in Argentina. However, any thoughts of superiority the boys may have harboured after that success were extinguished in Suva. We went down to a Western Fiji team in the quarterfinals and, just as it had been the year before, knew there was still plenty to be done before Hong Kong.

It was a younger side than the one I had taken there in 1994: Joeli Vidiri made his debut at 22 years of age; Adrian Cashmore, who I had first selected for Bay of Plenty in 1992, was a part of the side and was still just 21; Jonah was 19, as was Christian Cullen, Brad Fleming and the big Auckland loose forward Andrew Blowers. In fact, if it wasn't for Peter, Eric, Dallas and Joe, it may well have been the youngest team ever to tour. As it was, the average age was two years younger than it had been when I first took the team. It was to be a sign of things to come, but in future years my selection of younger players was more a result of having no other option.

Fortunately, I did have options in 1995, and it was tougher than the year before to settle on final selections for Hong Kong. I took a punt on the youngsters, knowing that they had all been unbelievable in training and would be anchored by Eric, Peter, Joe and Dallas. They would go on to win a second consecutive championship in Hong Kong, playing some of the best sevens I had ever seen. So balanced was the starting seven in that tournament that Christian Cullen only got one match, during which he scored the first try of the tournament and kicked six conversions. That I could leave him on the sideline for the rest of the tournament said less about him than it did about the guys starting.

We once again faced Fiji in the final and this time blew them away with a second-half onslaught. We had trailed 17–14 late in the first half, but the vision and composure of Peter and Eric, along with Jonah's unbelievable running game, saw us pile on 21 unanswered points to secure the trophy. Jonah was awarded the best and fairest player of the tournament, a rich reward for the effort he had put in during the training camps, and then he was offered to me for a tournament in Japan, in the middle of two games that would decide who made the All Blacks' Rugby World Cup team.

I couldn't believe what I was hearing. Here was this kid who was capable of the most extraordinary things on a rugby field and yet he was apparently unwanted even as a triallist for the All Blacks. It made absolutely no sense to me. I had seen him flourish in the sevens team, under the tutelage of our leaders, and he was the absolute star of the Hong Kong tournament in the eyes of everyone there. On the one hand, I was thrilled that he would be able to be a part of my team for the Japan tournament the following month, but it wasn't where he wanted to be. He wanted to be an All Black, and he damn well should have been.

I felt a sense of obligation to Jonah and, still struggling to come to terms with his supposed omission, I phoned a journalist and told him what I had heard. The following weekend he ran a story in the paper saying Jonah was not going to make the New Zealand trials. That year there were two games planned – a shadow trial under the banner of a North Island vs South Island fixture, and a further 'Probables vs Possibles' match two weeks later. It wasn't long before I received a phone call from an irate Laurie Mains. He had guessed I must have been the one to let slip the news, and he was far from pleased.

I couldn't understand why he was angry. If he didn't want Jonah in the side then that was his prerogative. The newspaper article was only reporting that decision. Surely he was comfortable with it? Whether he was, or wasn't, is up for debate. What is not is this: Jonah turned out in both games, scoring two tries in each, earned selection for the Rugby World Cup alongside Eric Rush and, once there, he stunned the world, ensured rugby turned professional overnight, and became the biggest name in the game.

Meanwhile, missing Eric, Dallas and Jonah in Japan, Fiji were able to avenge their Hong Kong loss and defeat us in the final. If there was a silver lining it came in the form of Christian Cullen, who played all five games, scored nine tries and amassed 89 points. I was rapt that Eric and Jonah were able to earn a World Cup spot, but we certainly missed them in the sevens squad. Following the nutrition theme, I guess you can't have your cake and eat it, too. And in sevens, there is always room for a slice of humble pie.

8

GROUND-
LEVEL
VIEWING

OVER THE FIRST two years, I felt that I had been able to develop a system for sevens coaching that got genuine and tangible results. When we first came together in 1994 the players had no idea about what was required, and in fairness I was flying somewhat by the seat of my pants, too. I knew I had to get them fit, I understood the fundamentals of the testing I subjected them to, and then I just figured they needed to run. Everything else had been built around conditioning and culture, and back-to-back Hong Kong titles had given me confidence in what I was doing.

I had wanted to create that culture based on traditional values: humility, respect, discipline, leadership and humour. It is often overlooked that having fun is a big thing in a team, and my two veterans in the side, Eric Rush and Dallas Seymour, always had a way to stay positive, even in the most intense session. They knew that the team together achieves more, and it was always about 'we' and never about 'I' with those two men. They were incredibly proud to be a part of the team and that was the key – for those players, that jersey meant everything. With that passion came enjoyment, and with that enjoyment came unity.

In sevens, that unity creates a family environment in which players genuinely care for the others in the side. Being smaller in numbers than a fifteens team meant we were closer, in camp and on tour. In turn, that closeness created a collective work ethic that revolved around self-motivation. Everyone in the team knew it was going to take hard work to win, and no one wanted to shirk that responsibility and let the team down. Eric was the one who led that in every respect. If he sensed a player wasn't giving their all to the cause, he would tell them. No one ever argued with Eric. He was the kaumatua, or elder statesman, pure and simple.

We were a team that brought a discipline to everything we did, and that also went for what we drank and what we ate. I had impressed upon the players, with the assistance of Jeni Pearce, the need for a high-performance diet, and the need to make sacrifices in order to win. That was the language of the day, of course. Over time, the word 'sacrifice' would disappear from the coaching lexicon. It would be replaced by the word 'choice'. Either way, my players could choose to eat burgers, or they could choose to win trophies.

I had seen players make great strides in those first couple of years, and it gave me tremendous confidence to see them coming into camps already at the level of fitness required. It showed me that messages were sinking in, that they cared about the team, and were passionate about performance. A coach gets great joy from knowing players are on programme when they are away from your environment, and the new players in the team see how much work is required of them. Succession leads to success.

All of this – the training, the discipline and the team culture – meant I had earned the players' respect, too. They knew that what I was going to offer them was consistency. It was one rule for all, and one level of expectation. We would never drop our standards to accommodate the weakest member of the squad. Instead we would all make an effort to bring that player up to the standard that was required of them. For the first couple of years I had the nation's most talented players at my disposal, which certainly made the job much easier. In 1996, with the advent of Super Rugby, I knew I was going to have to search far deeper than before.

―――――

Before Super Rugby, I was confident that I could go to the provincial tournaments and the nationals and find the likes of Glen Osborne and Christian Cullen and Eric Rush. Provincial rugby at the time didn't overlap with the sevens programme and as such there were no hurdles to selection. I could pick a squad, subject them to testing and a training camp, and then pick my team to travel. Suddenly, there were five franchises in the country, all selecting from the same pool of players, and they took precedence over sevens in every way. We had struck an agreement that I could have certain Super Rugby players released for Hong Kong, but even that was problematic.

I remember having an absolute battle with Peter Thorburn. He was the selection commissioner at the time and had an issue with my selection of Christian Cullen, who was signed to the Hurricanes in 1996. We were about to board a bus from Tauranga to Auckland in order to take our flight to Hong Kong when he rang to tell me that I should be releasing Christian Cullen for a Super Rugby match between the Hurricanes and Queensland instead. He wanted Christian to play the game, then join the rest of the team in Hong Kong just a few days before the tournament started. I flatly refused. For starters, I didn't want a team that had different rules for different players, and I also didn't want to risk Christian staying behind and suffering an injury in a game of fifteens when he was so crucial to my side.

I was not flavour of the month but I had to hold my ground. I was selecting a New Zealand team and I believed that that should always take precedence over what amounted to professional club rugby. Christian went on to be the star of the tournament (and the Hurricanes were defeated by Queensland), but more importantly, we had made a statement about where the national sevens side deserved to sit in the pecking order. It was a very vocal phone call, as I recall, with a few choice words thrown in for good measure. I could understand that the union had invested heavily in Super Rugby, but the call was especially ironic coming from a guy who had coached the sevens side to a World Cup.

When Christian Cullen lit up Hong Kong that year I was absolutely thrilled that I had been staunch on his selection. It was the most breathless individual display you could imagine. In the first game of the tournament he scored a record 37 points, including seven tries, and by the time the tournament had finished he had added records for the most tries (18) and the most points (136) in Hong Kong history. He was awarded the best and fairest player trophy, following in the footsteps of Glen Osborne and Jonah Lomu, and had announced his arrival on the world stage. This was the guy, you'll recall, who had featured in just one game in the previous year's tournament. The team was thrilled for him, and so was I.

When I had first met him the year before, I was struck by how quiet he was. I swear I barely heard him say a word in training or around the team environment. Originally, I thought he was shy, but as I got to know him and meet his family, I realised he was just incredibly humble. As he became more comfortable in the team, he began to come out of his shell, and when he was at the peak of his powers, as he was in that 1996 tournament, he was such an on-field presence that the ball always found its way to him. That's what sevens does for a young player – it creates a confidence born of effort and trust. There was no better support player in the game than Christian. He was always the guy there to take the final pass. Importantly, every other player knew he would be there.

What made that performance so special was that he was surrounded by other stars and still managed to shine. Jonah, Eric and Joe Tauiwi all played every game of that tournament and each one of them was influential in each of them. Christian was the icing on the top, the player who brought that little bit extra to bedazzle opponents. If they were marking Jonah or Waisake Masirewa, Christian found space. If they were marking Christian (and not many could), the others were scoring instead. It was further evidence that my selection policies were working. I had spotted the kid the year before on the back field at Palmerston North and 12 months later he was tearing the world apart. He was what every coach looks for when they are spotting for talent, and after that tournament, finding players like him became a full-time obsession.

I knew that if I wanted to maintain a level of success with the team, I would need to unearth sevens players who were going to be available to the programme. It was easier said than done, given the fact most players harboured ambitions to make it to Super Rugby and beyond. I was well aware of that, and just as Warwick Talbut had never held me back from pursuing my passion in sport, I didn't want to hold anyone back from their ambitions in rugby. Jonah Lomu, Joeli Vidiri, Adrian Cashmore, Eric Rush, and soon enough Christian Cullen, would all go on to represent the

All Blacks, and that gave me a great deal of satisfaction. The fact remained, however, that sevens was being squeezed for resources. I needed players.

I had tried earlier in the year to repeat what I had done in 1995, taking a mix of younger players and more experienced campaigners to tournaments in Uruguay and Fiji. Again, results had been mixed, with victory in South America followed by an agonising 21–22 defeat against the Fijians in Suva. Apart from wondering what it was going to take to win in Fiji, I was convinced that we were a team that needed the perfect balance to succeed. We'd had it in Hong Kong, pipping Fiji 19–17, but with the Super Rugby players unavailable for the following tournament in Japan, we were crushed 61–5 by Fiji in the final. It remains one of the heaviest, if not the heaviest, defeat of my career. Unfortunately, it would serve as a warning of what was to come.

We had gone to Japan without Christian, Jonah, Waisake, Eric, Dallas, Glen Osborne and Peter Woods. In short, we had gone without the bulk of our best starting line-up. The result showed me that unless we started to create a secondary core of starters, we were going to be massively on the back foot. The following year was the Sevens World Cup in Hong Kong. We needed as much depth as we could muster.

I have always watched games at ground level. It's the only place from which you can get a genuine sense of a player's talent for sevens. You can hear if they are a communicator – one of the key attributes of any of the game's greatest players. You can watch them organising players around them, thinking ahead of the game in moves beyond the ken of the opposition. At ground level, players look more powerful, bigger than they may first seem when you look at them on a screen or from the stands. And it's not just a simple matter of perspective. At ground level, you can hear and feel the contact, divine an awareness of a player's strength in the tackle or ability over the ball. You can also see the fatigue. It was important for me to be at ground level as much as possible once Super Rugby came to fruition. This was going to be my seat for the show, my window to a world of new talent. If I was going to find players who fit the bill, I was going to find them while sitting on the sideline and watching every minute of the action. At nationals the following year, I vowed not to miss a minute of play. It was a Sevens World Cup year and I needed as much back-up as I could muster.

I considered my presence at tournaments to be a crucial part of the job. It signified to players that I was there and I was watching. They deserved to know that whether it was a club tournament in the back of beyond, or a national championship, the door was open to anyone with ability at any level. I believed that by being there, I could legitimise their participation in the sport. If I couldn't make it to tournaments, I made sure I had someone on the ground who could give me an accurate scouting report, or watch certain players that I had my eye on. At nationals, I would take up residence on a plastic chair at the halfway line and stay there all day. It was always the same, lathered up in sunscreen, hat on the head, glasses on the face and most often lunch on the lap (chicken and salad). I'm sure I cut rather a lonely figure sitting there on my own but it was the only way I could focus. If others joined me, I would invariably get into a conversation and thus be distracted from the game. In sevens, moments are what make the difference. If I missed something, I wouldn't get another chance. There were no replays at this stage, and video analysis was still in its infancy in New Zealand.

I took a lot of phone calls from different coaches around the country, giving me tips on certain players, and as much as I could, I would get in my car and go and have a look at them. Sometimes they weren't at the level required, but I made a point of watching them and having a conversation with them, and I always remembered something about them. There were times when those very players were given an opportunity further down the track. The players in the team, too, became great mines of information. It didn't matter if a player was in the same position as them, if they had seen someone perform, they would ask me to go take a look at them. That was an unbelievable team-first mentality. Think about that: these guys were openly inviting me to go take a look at a player who could well end up taking their spot. It didn't matter. They wanted to be playing with the best players in the country and there were countless times when a player's recommendation led to a selection of a new guy in the side.

More often than not, I would go to tournaments with a plan to watch two or three players that I had my eye on. I always wanted to see guys play in more than one tournament before I picked them in my team, so often would plan my schedule around the events I knew they would be at. It made sense to go with just a couple of names in mind because if anyone else who was not on your radar stands out, in sevens you notice them anyway. I would watch for what they did with the ball and more often what they did without the ball. Sevens is a game of space with no time. The right running line in support, or the ability to create a diversion, can be the difference between the winning play and the losing feeling.

I would often be sent nomination forms from provincial coaches ahead of the nationals. I always appreciated the effort that went into those, but I admit I usually filed them away and only looked at them as I was mulling over my selections to see if my thinking was aligned with theirs. They were reference tools and they all mattered, but often I didn't want my thinking clouded before I took up residence on that plastic chair at the halfway line. What I was most looking for was a spark, what you may call an X-factor. Every good player can catch and pass, and can tackle, but the ones that really stand out in sevens are the guys who have that one little thing that sets them apart: the step, the acceleration, the vision, aerial skills, attacking nous. It could be as simple as hitting hard at the breakdown, or being able to repeat speed over and over throughout a tournament. They also had to have a work ethic. I have had challenges over the years with players who have had natural talent but no self-motivation. I have had others who could train the house down but didn't have the secret ingredient required for success at the highest level. The ones that had both – they were what I was searching for.

———

Unfortunately, in 1997 I would be unable to select a team at the national championships. In a World Cup year, the event had been moved from March to November, meaning it would be played well after the Cup. I was going to have to pick my squad on faith, instinct and a whole lot of help. It was, in hindsight, a preposterous decision in such an important year, but if I thought that was the only issue to contend with, I was very much mistaken.

I knew I had to build depth in a hurry ahead of the World Cup but there was only one tournament available to us, back in Suva at the scene of so much disappointment already. I had to take a punt on a bunch of young players, hoping that several of them would show me enough to warrant selection for the big tournament, which was being held in Hong Kong for the first time. Captained by Owen Scrimgeour, the team made it through to the semifinals, bowing out early once again, this time at the hands of Western Samoa. I wasn't overly disheartened, considering only Peter Woods and Joe Tauiwi of my big-name starters had made the trip. The others were unavailable because of Super Rugby commitments. I was also buoyed by the form of youngsters Karl Tenana and Rua Tipoki, and both men would make the team for the World Cup. Karl had played the World Cup qualifying tournament the year before, while Rua was a gifted playmaker. If I could put them in a side packed with real sevens ability, there was no reason they couldn't shine on the world stage. That was the plan, anyway.

The reality was vastly different. Dallas Seymour, who had been plagued with injury that season, was invalided out of contention, while Jonah, Christian, Adrian Cashmore and the speedster Brad Fleming were also ruled out. Waisake Masirewa and Joeli Vidiri were not available due to the fact both men had represented Fiji in the past. Suddenly, three and a half years of hard work and fine-tuning seemed more like a crap shoot and a lucky dip. I was genuinely concerned that we just wouldn't have enough firepower to win the pinnacle event on the calendar. I couldn't betray that anxiety to the players, though. We had built a team based on trust and that was a two-way street. I had selected the best team I could from the players available and now we had to go out and deliver.

We easily accounted for Japan and Tonga in pool play, leaning heavily on the pace of a kid by the name of Caleb Ralph, who would go on to play 104 consecutive games for the Crusaders in Super Rugby, and Glen Osborne and Roger Randle. In the quarterfinal, we were also able to outrun the Australians for a comfortable win. However, in the semifinal, against a powerful South African team, we came up way too short, managing just one try in a 7–31 defeat. I was crushed by the result, and the players were too. We had been able to achieve so much in a short space of time and yet in many ways it felt like we were back at square one again. I wondered if I would be better leaving the job and concentrating full-time on the Bay of Plenty side, but there was something else just around the corner that I couldn't resist: the first-ever sevens tournament at a Commonwealth Games.

I didn't want to leave the job with any regrets, and the Commonwealth Games presented the kind of challenge I needed to get back on the horse and go again. I had always chased my dreams in the past, and I could do so again, leaving the nightmare of the World Cup behind me. I realised we had been undone by a particularly debilitating combination of a lack of preparation and an injury toll that few, if any, teams would have been able to deal with. What I didn't know – couldn't possibly know – was that in the very distant future a similar set of circumstances would conspire to derail us at the biggest tournament in sevens history.

9

HEADACHES AND MEDALS

FROM THE MOMENT that I selected my first New Zealand team, I knew I was tasked with making big calls. In that first team for Hong Kong I included three Bay of Plenty players, against the wishes of others on the selection panel at the time. They all delivered for me on the field, which I was eternally grateful for. They were instinctive calls at the time, and they were the right decisions to make. I believed that trusting my gut would almost always be the best thing to do when it came to selecting teams.

In 1997, I had selected a New Zealand team to play against a New Zealand Fijian team. By now, I should have been aware of how good Fijian players were at every level, but if I had any lingering doubts they were soon extinguished. There was one player in that Fijian team who absolutely tore us apart that day. His name was Amasio Valence Raoma. He had what every great Fijian player had: the ability to buy time. He was so composed that he was never under pressure, no matter how well we adjusted our defensive line to combat him. I had to find out who he was, and soon discovered he was still at Sacred Heart College in Auckland. I called the school and asked them to put Amasio through a beep test, a standardised series of shuttle runs that measure an athlete's maximum oxygen uptake, and aerobic capacity. Amasio reached level 13 in the test, well above the average result for his age. I needed no further evidence. I selected him in my squad there and then. He went on to win three Commonwealth gold medals with the New Zealand side and become one of the all-time great playmakers in World Rugby Sevens Series history. He was a guy spotted quite by accident and picked on nothing but instinct.

In business, too, many of the calls around staffing that I have made have been based on feel. I do wonder why more people don't listen to their instinct in everyday life. We know inherently what we want and how we need to go about achieving it, but all too often we silence the one voice that is telling us to go out and do it. We have become overly reliant on data, clouding brains that are already overstimulated in everyday life. The best people decisions I have ever made have been ones based on good old-fashioned gut feel.

Rob O'Sullivan is the Revenue Manager at Bay Engineers and has been with the company for almost 15 years. He first started on the counter for us, and was routinely promoted over time. He is one of the hardest working guys we have, a mine of information with a deep empathy for staff and a passion for the business. I take great pride in knowing I asked Rob to join the company all those years ago. At the time he was the guy who filled my car with petrol at the local service station.

Holly Davies is one of the best sales reps we have at our company. When she first started with us she knew nothing about engineering supplies and had no formal sales qualifications. Like Rob, she started slowly and with each passing year has become more and more valuable to the company. I also take a lot of pride in the fact I offered her a job with us. At the time she was serving me coffee at a cafe in Mount Maunganui.

What both Rob and Holly showed me was an infectious

enthusiasm for their jobs, an abiding respect for their customers and a wonderful energy that was irresistible to everyone around them. I knew they would make everyone they came into contact with feel cherished, and in our line of work that counts for so much. I employed them not because of their CVs or their qualifications, but because they were impressive people. I employed them because my gut instinct told me they would add something to our business. In rugby and in life, people like Rob and Holly are always the standouts.

However, while gut instinct was key to selecting both players and people, and had served me well over my short career as New Zealand coach, it was much harder to trust when you had to tell those same players that they were not in the team – as I was about to discover. The 1998 Commonwealth Games in Kuala Lumpur would be the litmus test for me in this department. I had one chance to get my selections right, and there was going to be a lot of emotional pain along the way.

We had put behind us the mistakes of the year before and loaded our preparation for Kuala Lumpur with competitive tournaments. The 1997 World Cup had taught us all a lesson in the value of sevens-specific fitness and the need to have readily available back-ups in the event of an injury catastrophe. We also arranged to have 20 players on sevens contracts. They were badly needed to ensure we had access to players, and that they were committed to the sevens programme. From December 1997 through to the Commonwealth Games in September 1998, we played in 10 tournaments, taking us from Dubai to South America, Sydney,

Fiji, Hong Kong, Japan, Paris and – of all places – Jerusalem.

We weren't always successful – and again the Hong Kong title eluded us – but as much as we hated to lose, we were taking every opportunity to develop our game, and to build that all-important team unity. There were going to be no 'what ifs' in Kuala Lumpur. At least, that was what I hoped. The contracting of players gave me something I had always wanted in the team: competition for places. Every time we assembled for training, or for a tournament, guys were stepping up, doing everything they could to make the team. It forced every player to be 100 per cent focused on doing everything right – staying fit, eating well, being supportive of other team members and respectful of the environment they were a part of. It felt like everything was on track for us, and then we lost one of our own.

Richard Crawshaw had been our manager as we traversed the globe playing build-up tournaments to the Commonwealth Games. A real estate man from Gisborne, 'Craw' was a sensational manager with a keen eye for detail and an amazing rapport with the players. We got on exceptionally well. I spent many hours bouncing ideas around with him, and his presence gave me peace of mind that every logistical detail would be covered. He was incredibly professional and we were very lucky to have him. Unfortunately, Richard passed away after a battle with cancer just a month before the Games were to begin. His death, though incredibly sad for everyone, galvanised us as a team. Every player that could manage it made it to the funeral in Gisborne to pay their respects. I was enormously proud of the guys that day and I know it meant a lot to Craw's family that we all made the effort to attend. His replacement, Ross Thurston, would go on to do an amazing job for us, too.

Alas, there was to be one more hurdle to jump in the lead-up to the competition. In that same month, Eric Rush had borrowed Glen Osborne's car to drive from Rotorua to Auckland. Driving in terrible conditions, he failed to take a corner and collided with another vehicle. The driver was killed in the crash, and Eric was devastated. It was an unimaginable tragedy for the family of the man whose life was lost in that wreck, and it had a deep and lasting impact on Eric, who would take a long time to come to terms with what had happened. He was also injured in the accident, though I could tell that that was the least of his concerns. As a high-profile athlete, the media coverage was relentless, and the sense of guilt Eric felt was at times overwhelming. We wanted to support him as best we could, knowing that the place he belonged was with us in the team. I didn't know what shape he was going to be in mentally, or physically, but I knew – in my gut – that we had to give him every chance to be a part of the Games. If we cut him loose, he might never be able to get through that terrible time.

Having endured more than enough tragedy by the time we left for our training camp in Singapore, we were desperate to get back into our work and put our campaign back on a positive footing. Eric would travel with us, needing to prove his fitness – both in body and in mind – before he could be selected. And it would not be easy. Singapore was hot, steamy and inarguably the hardest training camp the team had ever been through. All up, 15 players had been chosen to travel but only 10 could be selected for the Games. The strain placed on them would be a test of everything we had built as a team; it would challenge every player's resilience and character. It would also be a test of everything I thought was required from a coach and a selector.

The one thing I never wanted to do was pick a team on emotion. Instinct and emotion are two very different things. In the course of my career, many of my selections would have been very different if they had been controlled by emotion. Instead, I made sure I did my homework and that my thinking was clear, so clearing a path for the selection instinct to do its job. It was never an easy thing to make a call between two very good players, but it was the reality of the role. In the back of your mind you are thinking, 'Man, that guy is pretty good, and this is a massive call', but you have to possess the strength of character to override that. It is an instinct, developed over a long period of time, and it is your greatest asset in life, in work and in sport.

The players understand from a professional point of view that I have that job, and that those decisions are mine to make, but that doesn't mean they have to like every call, and there will be some hurt feelings along the way. Eric Rush always told the story of his father who would say to him every time he missed out on a rep team, 'It's only one man's opinion, son.' When Eric made the All Blacks in 1995 and broke the news to his father, he replied, 'It's only one man's opinion, son.' I could see where Eric got his sense of humour from. There was nothing humorous about the task ahead of me, though. On the positive side, Eric came through the week adequately enough to ensure he would captain the team at the Commonwealth Games. It was a great result for him after the pain of the previous month. He had to get there the hard way, too. He may have been the leader of the team, but he was not going to get a free ride into such an important tournament. Five other men, however, would not be so lucky. And they needed to be told face to face.

Even though I had a clear plan in my head around who should

make that team, I still sought some third-party counsel, just to be absolutely certain I was on the right track. Keith Roberts, who had been with me for several years as my fitness trainer, was one person I spoke with at length. He knew the guys well, understood all of their capabilities, and, like me, was a devotee of testing data and plenty of time spent running. If anyone could bring a purely scientific point of view to proceedings it was him. I also consulted Eric. As leader, he had earned the right to have an opinion. Our conversations all led to the same conclusions, and on the morning of the team naming I called in each of the players in the squad. One by one they had to be told whether or not they had made the final cut for the Games.

They were devastatingly hard conversations to have with those who had missed, especially given each of them had performed well for me at other times. Yet, as tough as it was, I knew it would be completely unfair on a player to find out in a full team announcement that he was no longer required. It would have shown a lack of respect for the player's contribution and their emotional wellbeing. If you have got to the point at which that person has not performed for you, or that someone else is playing better than them, I believe the first person you need to address it with is the person most affected. Most often, that conversation should be well advanced even before the decision is made. There are always reasons that a player may be off form. It could be that they have been away from the environment, or that injury has curtailed their preparation, or that there are external factors that may be leading to a downgrade in their focus.

A coach should always be talking to those people who are most at risk of falling out of the selection picture, because only then will they know what it is they need to work on, and only then will you have a better understanding of what can be done to help them get better. In my time with the New Zealand team, that was something I prided myself on – my ability to have those conversations when necessary and to communicate with the players on the areas they needed to improve in. Being honest and upfront was always the best way to maximise what you had in the team, and get more out of those people who you knew could make a contribution.

No surprises. That should be the way a team operates. I had to earn the respect of the players and I could only do that if I was consistent, and consistently talked to them. I was there to make sure the team was the best it could be and that everyone in it was playing as well as they possibly could. That's the secret to long and steady success: always select the team you believe can go out and win. Time after time, what I learned from doing this is that the players know better than anyone else about where they are physically and mentally and how well they are playing. When they remove the emotion, they are just as capable as a coach – if not more so – of evaluating their true position.

I was relieved that the training camp was over and the hard job of selecting the team was done. We could now focus on getting to Kuala Lumpur and taking our shot at history. The team was champing at the bit to get to the athletes' village and to experience being part of a bigger New Zealand team. We had become so used to operating in our own little bubble that my only concern was the guys wouldn't know what to do with themselves in a village of 6000 other athletes. Or perhaps the concern was more that they *would* know what to do with themselves!

As it was, we had to keep our minds firmly on the task ahead. Not surprisingly, players such as Jonah and Christian garnered their fair share of attention from fellow athletes at the Games. It was good for them and the rest of the team to realise that they were held in such high regard by participants in other sports, and it was only right that they got to enjoy the moment. We were still there to do a job, though, and it was not long before we were back into action, and ready for the first day of competition.

Though it had been a fraught process selecting the team, I could not have been more pleased with the players we had in Kuala Lumpur. We had the leaders of the team, our foundation players, Eric Rush and Dallas Seymour; we had the express pace of Caleb Ralph, Christian Cullen, Bruce Reihana, Roger Randle and Rico Gear; we had the unbelievable game-breaking ability of Jonah Lomu and Joeli Vidiri; and we had the preternaturally gifted playmaker Amasio Valence Raoma. It was a team that could play the game at a breakneck speed. And that's exactly what I believed was going to win us the gold medal.

Despite the confidence we had in our superior fitness, the tournament format was a great leveller for other teams. With just two games per day, sides who may not have been as well conditioned as us would have the benefit of the extra recovery time. For a team like Fiji, that was absolute gold, and we all knew it. The pool stages of play became a shootout between Australia and ourselves to see who could find a pathway to the final that avoided an early clash with the side we most feared. Despite racking up 268 combined points against Sri Lanka, Malaysia, Tonga and the Bahamas, our fate still rested with the final pool match between Australia and Sri Lanka. If they scored enough, they would force us into a semifinal showdown with Fiji.

I needed to stay to watch the game. The rest of the team had taken up residence in a nearby hotel where they could rest easily between matches, but I was pacing like a madman as the action unfolded before me. The Australians were scoring with ease against Sri Lanka, and I knew if they kept up the pace, they would achieve their goal. Wanting desperately to have the favourable draw, I offered some advice to the Sri Lankan coach: slow the game down. Needless to say, he agreed. The team followed his instructions and kicked the ball into the grandstands at every available opportunity, and the Australians didn't get quite enough points. I still remember the look of frustration on David Campese's face!

On 14 September, we headed into the day of the finals. There was a real nervousness among the boys, which I wasn't overly worried about. We had a clear and concise plan, some of the best players in the game, and we had done all the hard work leading into the event. Nervous though we were, I also knew we were prepared. Wales certainly had no answer in the quarterfinal. Jonah Lomu and Roger Randle combined for five tries and we were comfortably into the semifinal. Comfortably was not a word I would use to describe the next victory, though. Samoa were absolutely relentless and we only just scraped through with a 17–14 win.

We were now assured of a medal, but none of us would have been satisfied with silver. We were playing against Fiji for gold or bust. We had 20 minutes of sevens ahead of us to decide if we were going to be standing on top of the podium. It was a brutally hot evening, humid and stifling in the stadium, and between us and gold was a team that had tormented us over the previous two years.

We needed the performance of a lifetime, and we got it.

Sevens is nothing more than a collection of critical moments, and that final against Fiji was filled with all the tension it deserved. It took five energy-sapping minutes before Dallas Seymour collected a pass from Eric Rush for the first try of the match, and only a few minutes later the great Waisale Serevi stopped a certain try and set up one of his own at the other end of the field to level the scores. Christian Cullen eventually broke the deadlock just before the break, but we knew a seven-point lead was not going to be enough.

Fiji hit back after halftime, bringing the score to within two points. From there the game seemed to stretch into an eternity of half chances and near misses. In the end, Fiji's lack of discipline cost them dearly, and when Caleb Ralph somehow kicked through and regathered for a try with three minutes to go, we thought we had done enough. In those final, frenetic few minutes, we hung on to the ball, and the match, and for the first time in history New Zealand was the Commonwealth Games sevens champion.

It was a moment I would cherish for the rest of my life. Seeing the elation on the faces of those men was unforgettable, and to watch them atop the dais, as the anthem played and the New Zealand flag was hoisted behind them, was vindication for me both as a coach and a selector. I had been forced to make some tough calls, had trusted my instinct, and had picked the team to win. It felt as if I had arrived as a coach, as if everything I had been building over the last four years had finally paid off in the best possible way. All of the trainings, the endless shuttles and testing, the constant search for players, and the trust and faith I had in the leaders of that team had reaped the ultimate reward. At least, I thought it was the ultimate reward. As I was about to discover, there was plenty more just around the corner.

10

A NEW ERA

IN THE EARLY years of my time with New Zealand I believed we had been on the cutting edge of sevens in terms of preparation, discipline, diet and game plan. I knew we were the hardest-working team on the planet – not always the most gifted, but most definitely the hardest-working. We hadn't always achieved the results, but what we had won had real and tangible meaning. There were the three Hong Kong titles and the Commonwealth Games gold medal, not to mention a number of other titles that had largely been forgotten due to the low profile of the game outside the major tournaments of the year. All in all, it was a fair haul for a side that had firmly established itself at the forefront of the sport. Now I had to decide whether I had served my time. Was I prepared to keep going or was it someone else's turn to take the reins? Whoever was in charge would have to make sure that the programme continued to develop. Change was coming, and the sport was only going to get tougher.

You have to believe in what you are doing in life. If you take on any job half-heartedly you are setting yourself up to fail. No matter what I had done so far – in work or in sport – I had always given it maximum effort. If you do that, you are left with no regrets. If you give it your best shot, you have done all you can, and you can live with that win or lose. If you know you have short-changed yourself by not throwing everything you can muster at an opportunity, that will always haunt you. As the millennium drew to a close, I needed to once again reassess my 'why'. I had a young family, a thriving business to attend to, a Bay of Plenty side that was still languishing in second division and that desperately craved an elevation back to the top flight, and in front of me the prospect of a first-ever Sevens World Series. Did I have the energy to commit to all of those things at once? And if I did, was I prepared to do whatever it took to succeed?

Tactically and technically, I knew I had the trust in the players – that they were doing what was expected of them mentally and physically, and they understood that I was doing all I could to offer them every advantage they needed to perform. In business, Warwick Talbut was still absolutely behind my coaching aspirations and encouraged me to keep going. My family was infinitely supportive, even though the job meant many hours on the road and away from home. As for Bay of Plenty, I had told the union that it would take five years, and I still had one up my sleeve!

Ultimately, although everything else was in place to continue, it was once again going to be a choice that relied on instinct. I knew that there were going to be challenges ahead. I knew that the player availability issue was one that had very little chance of being resolved. I knew that with the advent of the World Series, other teams would eventually catch up to us in terms of their training and fitness regimes. I knew that there would be more big decisions ahead – another Sevens World Cup just around the corner, and perhaps another Commonwealth Games after that. Did I have the strength to go through those emotions with players again, perhaps on an even more regular basis?

I thought about all of this and kept coming back to the same conclusion. I absolutely loved coaching that sevens team, and loved the players in it. They had become my extended family, and I cared deeply about their future. I had been absolutely invigorated by the Commonwealth Games gold medal and desperately wanted to experience that high again. In short, it was where I knew I belonged. I signed on, grabbed my notebook, and set about planning the season ahead. I was in alright, balls and all.

———

There had been speculation for some time that a formalised world series was in the pipeline, but in all honesty, I hadn't put a lot of thought into it. When the idea was first floated, I was uncertain about whether I would be involved by the time something like that ever came to fruition. In the end, it came around faster than I imagined and, sure enough, here I was. It gave me pause for thought. How amazing it was to see how far sevens had come since I had first been introduced to the game back in the late 1970s.

The popularity of the game itself and the way in which it was providing the second-tier nations with a stage upon which to perform gave the concept some much-needed impetus. At the turn of the century, rugby was four years into professionalism and starting to see the benefit of the World Cup tournaments and the increased exposure of multinational competition. Many countries, however, were simply incapable of competing in the fifteen-a-side game. Sevens, then, was a great rugby leveller. Teams like Kenya and Japan were given a real opportunity to play against and beat some very good sides. The island nations had already proved that they had what it took to succeed at the very highest level. Sevens

I absolutely loved coaching that sevens team, and loved the players in it. They had become my extended family.

was all about entertainment – both on the field and off it – as Hong Kong had proved over a long period of time. There was a demand for similar events in other countries, especially those with an expat community such as Dubai, or developing rugby nations that wanted to cement the game in the hearts and minds of local fans. The best way to do that was to bring the game to them.

There was an appetite from the public to see games played by conditioned, expressive athletes who displayed wonderful skill sets and exceptional pace. That was exactly what I wanted to see, and once again the search for players was on. The success of the previous few years meant I could be confident in the methods we had in camp and in our lead-in to tournaments, and we wasted no time in looking to once again develop our player base before the World Series began. Between December 1998 and May 1999, the New Zealand Sevens team played in nine tournaments, reaching the final in each of them and winning six. It had been Fiji that had won the other three – in Hong Kong, Dubai and at their home event. By this stage I was wondering if a New Zealand team would ever taste victory in Suva, but I knew those losses had set the tone for what was to be a massive showdown ahead.

There is no doubt that the rivalry between the two nations was intense. To Fijians, sevens and religion go hand in hand. I had been there enough to know that they had a conveyer belt of ready-made players, all of them forged in the fires of village competitions in which teams could play up to nine games in a day. They were supremely fit, with a feel for the game like no other people on earth. The national players were heroes to the citizenry, and each victory gave them enormous pride. The team drew their inspiration from Philippians 4:13: 'I can do all things through Christ who strengthens me.' We, on the other hand, would have to draw our inspiration from 'Running 16:150'. Nothing had changed in terms of the basic fitness regime of our team. It was into camp for speed testing, followed by a phosphate decrement test, which measures a player's ability to repeat sprint speed through the effects of fatigue, followed by a beep test, and then rounded out by sixteen 150-metre sprints with 40-second rests. Everything else came on top of that basic set, and as much as it strained every cord of a player's being, it remained the ultimate test of endurance and character. If we were going to have more events, we were going to need to be fitter than we had ever been before. We were also going to have to be stronger.

The issue of scale was not one I was unaccustomed to. At Bay Engineers we had grown from one solitary office in 1983 to more than 10 by the turn of the century. Scale is simply a matter of organisation and people. When you see the opportunity for growth, you have to be agile enough to make the leap; and in order to make the leap, you have to find the appropriate people to provide the springboard. We had always managed to retain the core culture of the business no matter how big we became. We had some bottom lines in terms of our reputation and our team spirit that were non-negotiable. We did what we said we would do, we treated everyone with respect, we were invariably positive in how we approached problems, and we supported one another in every endeavour. It was the same with the sevens team. No matter how far the sport had come, it was still a team that relied on those original, traditional values: hard work, humility, respect and manners, gratitude and discipline. In essence, we were simply adding new branches, scaling up our operation while retaining our core purpose.

By the time we hit Dubai for the first-ever World Series event, we were ready to take our shot. We cruised through the tournament and defeated the Fijians with ease in the final. It was especially pleasing for me to have men like Brad Fleming and Rua Tipoki in that side. They were two of the players who had been cut just before the Commonwealth Games, and it was a testament to their character that they were back and ready to play for the team after such a personal disappointment.

———

Disappointing is one way to describe the following week when Fiji were able to reverse the Dubai result in Stellenbosch. The tournament was ours for the taking, but we lacked the killer instinct when it really counted and lost by just two points. The Fijians had found a new sense of purpose through the introduction of the World Series. I could tell that they desperately wanted to be crowned world champions after having their hearts shattered the year before. As the millennium dawned and we jetted off to Uruguay for the South American leg of the series, we all knew we were in the fight of our lives. Unfortunately, at the same time, my father was fighting for his life.

A genuine sense of helplessness sets in almost immediately when you receive bad news so far from home. When we landed in Buenos Aires, I got word that my dad was in intensive care back in New Zealand, and by the time we had taken our connecting flight and arrived in Punta del Este, he had passed away. There was nothing I could do but book the next available flight home and trust that my manager Tony Ward and the team knew what needed to be done. It may seem strange that at a time like that I was concerned about a sevens tournament, but that was my job and the work kept my mind off the loss. A couple of days after that long

Playing for Waikato against the British Lions, 1983. *Photosport*

A few of the New Zealand Sevens team after playing Singapore
in Hong Kong, 1983. L–R: Andrew Donald, Hika Reid, Richard Fry,
yours truly. *Sir Gordon Tietjens collection*

Jonah Lomu broke the sevens game wide open before going on to do the same in fifteens. Here I am with the big man, holding the World Cup, Argentina, 2001. *Sandra Teddy/Photosport*

Eric Rush was a highly effective leader of men and a player with massive heart. This photo was taken after we won gold at the 2002 Commonwealth Games in Manchester. *Sandra Teddy/Photosport*

DJ Forbes was my captain for 10 seasons, and became my Rushie Mk II. In this photo, I'm holding the IRB 7s World Series Trophy as DJ holds the London 7s Trophy, 11 May 2014. *Matthew Impey/Wired Photos*

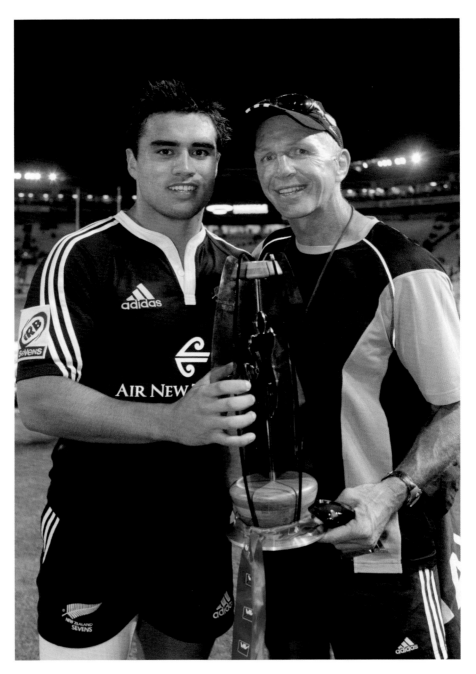

Liam Messam was always a fierce competitor in the sevens realm.
Here, we have just won the Wellington tournament in 2005.
Marty Melville/Photosport

Acknowledging the crowd after beating England 29–21 to win gold at the 2006 Commonwealth Games in Melbourne.
Hannah Johnston/Photosport

The 2016 Rio Olympics campaign was, and still is, such a huge disappointment for me – we should've done better. Here I am, aghast, after our loss to Japan. *John Cowpland/Photosport*

A new start – head coach of Samoa. Day 1 of the 2017 World Rugby Sevens series, at Westpac Stadium in Wellington. *John Cowpland/Photosport*

What an honour –
receiving my knighthood
from Lieutenant General
The Right Honourable
Sir Jerry Mateparae,
16 September 2013.
*Sir Gordon Tietjens
collection*

Tennis is a personal passion of mine. Here's the great Onny Parun
and me after a hit-out at the Renouf Tennis Centre in Wellington.
Sir Gordon Tietjens collection

My lovely wife Jules and best buddy Nugget, at our holiday haven in Ohope. *Sir Gordon Tietjens collection*

I couldn't be a prouder dad. My two children, Kylie and Paul. *Sir Gordon Tietjens collection*

journey home to say my farewells, I was on a plane once more and heading back to Uruguay. I arrived in time for the quarterfinal and watched as the boys cruised into the semi, and on to the final. They were men possessed in that tournament, and ended up closing out Fiji fantastically to win the event. I was humbled that they had put so much effort into winning. In my absence, I knew that Eric had led them superbly and never once allowed them to take their foot off the accelerator. It may have been just a sevens tournament, but that win carried such significance for the fact the boys had done all they could to win it, without me.

The joy was short-lived, and another loss was to follow in Argentina, again at the hands of Fiji. It seemed that every time we thought we had their measure they would find a way to surprise us. You couldn't prepare for the flair they brought to the game, and I was left with no choice but to keep fine-tuning our own style of play, hoping we could execute perfectly when it really mattered. It would certainly matter in the next event – our very first in front of our home fans.

The inaugural Wellington Sevens tournament provided our first chance to play in front of a home crowd, and that really did mean everything to us as a team, knowing that our families and friends were there experiencing that event with us. We were absolutely rapt to finally be playing at home, and the NZRFU were very keen to make sure the tournament was a success, releasing Jonah Lomu and Christian Cullen from Super Rugby duties to give the Wellington event some genuine star appeal. I was happy to have their services, and having become accustomed to having to select players from outside franchises, their return to the sevens fold was a welcome one. Unfortunately, my worst fears were realised as soon as they joined us in camp. They were going to battle to be sevens fit in time for the tournament. I knew I wanted them to be a part of the team; I knew what they were capable of doing on the field; but I could see that they were nowhere near as conditioned to play as I needed them to be.

Although Jonah had never been a great trainer, his X-factor was so massive that you could trust him to get through a game and do something special. He had been unbelievable in the Commonwealth Games final, but that fact notwithstanding, I knew this was going to be a struggle for him. I picked both men in the squad for Wellington, but I would only play them off the bench. I had to be consistent and fair on the other guys in the team. No one was bigger than that, not even two of the all-time greats.

I would come in for a fair share of criticism by playing them off the bench – even more so when we lost the final to Fiji. I was dismissive of that, knowing full well that over the last four years I had seen my theories on sevens-specific fitness validated time and time again. Critics saw the headline names and failed to understand the underlying story. It would be a constant battle in the years to come, trying to convince people that the two versions of the game weren't as interchangeable as everyone thought. A sevens player could more easily move to fifteens than a fifteens player could move to sevens. Of that I was convinced, and remain so to this day.

The Fijians had loved winning in Wellington, especially as they had taken us down in the final. Such was the nature of the rivalry that year that we had a chance to exact the sweetest revenge on them the following week in Suva. I had never won a title in Fiji as a coach in any event. A win in Fiji would be right up there with any Hong Kong title I had won in the past given the fact I thought it the toughest place in which to win. We once again made it through to the final, thanks in large part to the outstanding play of Karl Tenana, who seemed able to score almost at will. He was well assisted in that department by a young Mils Muliaina, who would later go on to be capped 100 times for the All Blacks. The two men were sensational in the final, scoring a brace apiece and leading us to a first-ever Fijian win.

Over the next few months the World Series lead continued to swing between us and the Fijians. We only missed one final all year – in Brisbane where we were defeated by the home side in the semifinals – and that was enough to allow the Fijians to get the jump on us in terms of series points. We backed that up by reclaiming the Hong Kong title, only to lose the following tournament in Japan. Everything would come down to the final event of the series, in Paris that May. If Fiji made the final, the series was theirs.

It is hard to express just how nerve-wracking that French tournament was. On the one hand, we had a team that knew exactly what it needed to do: win at all costs. On the other, we were constantly watching the Fijians, hoping beyond hope that somehow they would be tripped up along the way to the sudden-death section. If their team motto was 'I can do all things through Christ who strengthens me', this time ours was 'Lord help us'. It turns out that, every once in a while, a prayer is answered. Argentina, somehow, managed to beat the Fijians in the quarterfinal. We now had a chance to claim the whole damn thing.

A sevens player could more easily move to fifteens than a fifteens player could move to sevens. Of that I was convinced, and remain so to this day.

Over the next three matches, that team did everything that was asked of it, first defeating the home side in the quarters, then Australia in the semis, and finally wiping the floor with South Africa in the final. It was a statement win to finish the year, a 69–10 hammering to put the final nail in the coffin. I don't know whether divine intervention played a part, whether my father was smiling down on us that day in Paris, but I do know this: being crowned World Series champions was a career-defining moment for those boys, and for once I relaxed my stance. If ever there was cause to celebrate, this was most certainly it.

It was the start of a golden age for the New Zealand Sevens team, and before too long attention had returned to the small matter of the Sevens World Cup. It was one title that had eluded us over the years, and we desperately wanted to add it to the trophy cabinet. Rugby World Cup wins had become rather elusive for New Zealand in all forms of the game – apart from women's rugby where the Black Ferns had become a dominant force. The All Blacks had failed in their last three attempts to once again lift the William Webb Ellis Cup, and in 2001 we had the chance to make some positive World Cup headlines.

It was set to be a big year for me personally. After the World Series win in 2000, I had returned to coaching Bay of Plenty in that year's second-division championship. Clayton McMillan had come through from my time with the Colts to lead the full representative side, and a number of my sevens squad members, including Rico Gear, Justin Wilson and Craig de Goldi, showed the benefits of superior fitness, making an impact all season long. We had a great pack – strong and aggressive – and a backline that was capable of launching an attack from anywhere. We only lost twice that season – first in a pre-season fixture against North Harbour, and once in the championship against Marlborough. We would end up playing and beating old rivals King Country in a high-scoring semifinal, and then avenge our final defeat from the previous year against Nelson Bays. With the second-division title finally in the bag, and an expanded first division planned for 2001, Bay of Plenty were back in the big show at last. I was only sorry it had taken six seasons, not the five I had promised.

As thrilled as I was to see the Bay back in the top flight, I didn't have time to dwell on that. The new World Series was scheduled to start in November in Durban and Dubai, and the demands of the series coupled with the World Cup in January forced us to build a veritable army of sevens players, many of whom were only just embarking on their journey in professional rugby. There had been hours of planning put in around which Super Rugby players with sevens pedigree would be available and for how long, even more time spent on identifying up-and-coming talent, and there was also an imperative to give my sevens specialists as much game time as I could.

We seemed to have struck on a winning formula right from the start, winning both in Durban and in Dubai. We were developing a new, aggressive style that other teams were finding hard to combat. There was a new generation of gifted loose forwards emerging in the professional system and I was keen to get my hands on as many of them as possible, especially as my old pro Dallas Seymour was battling with form and fitness – not surprisingly, given he had been playing at the top level of the game for 15 seasons. So we headed to the World Cup in January 2001 feeling confident in our game plan and personnel. Jonah had been able to rejoin the team and get himself into the best possible shape, while Mils Muliaina and Karl Tenana were both at the peak of their powers. We were also bolstered by young bucks Craig Newby and Rodney So'oialo who provided much-needed muscle at the breakdown. And we still had our kaumatua, Eric Rush. That was until the final pool game of the tournament. In that 17–7 gritty win over England, Eric broke his leg.

I cannot tell you how devastating that was for Eric, and for the team. For so many seasons that champion man had given every ounce of his being for the team. He had been my trusted advisor, my most valuable leader, and undoubtedly the most beloved and respected man in the squad. Watching him being stretchered off during that game took the wind out of everyone's sails, mine included. All I could do was get the team into a huddle and settle them down. They knew what to do, and they didn't need to be told. I wasted no time in elevating Karl Tenana to the captaincy, both on form and because he had been close to Eric and had learned so much from him. The boys – especially Jonah – were torn apart at the fate which had befallen Eric, who was nevertheless doing his best to hold it together. He knew this would have been his final shot at a World Cup title, and although he put on a brave face for the team, that visage crumbled the next day when the boys sent him home, full cast and all, with a full-blown haka. From that moment, I knew we couldn't lose. We simply had to win for our captain.

Over the next three matches, I watched boys come of age in the black jersey, and a legend reaffirm his place among the greats. Eric's early exit had provided all the motivation those guys required to sweep aside Samoa in the quarters, hosts Argentina in the semis, and finally Australia in the trophy match. Jonah, channelling all of his despair and resolve, scored a hat trick in the final, and the Mundialista Stadium crowd erupted every time he touched the ball. By full-time we were convincing winners, 31–12. More importantly, we were world champions. No one could take that away from us for four more years. I would have loved Eric to have that moment, to be able to stand there and raise that trophy above his head. He never got the chance. I know, however, that he got something just as special: an entire team that went out that day and did it just for him. That shows just what a champion he was.

With the World Series now taking up seven months of the year, I decided that 2001 would be my last year with the Bay of Plenty side. I wanted one chance to coach in the first division and this would be it. Despite winning our opening match of the first-division season against defending champions Wellington, and pushing Auckland to the limit the following week, the elevation proved challenging for the side in its first season back. By the end of the year, we had collected just two first-division victories and were forced into a promotion/relegation match with Hawke's Bay. Fortunately, we came out on top with a 32–12 victory in front of our home fans in Rotorua.

My Bay of Plenty journey had come full circle. I ended my tenure there having played for the Bay of Plenty on 81 occasions and having coached the senior side for seven seasons. They were back in the first division, where I always thought they belonged. It may not have always been pretty but I was a loyal Bay man and I had been enormously proud to play for and to coach that side. Many a good man came through those teams, and the Steamers will always have a special place in my heart. For now, though, it was obvious that my heart belonged elsewhere. It was time to devote all my attention to sevens.

PART THREE

—

LEAVING A LEGACY

11

—

ALL THE HELP I COULD GET

I NEVER THOUGHT I was doing any of this on my own. Although I'm writing about my own career, I wouldn't have been able to achieve anything had it not been for a remarkable support team in every area of my life: family, business and sport. It is so important to surround yourself with highly capable and energetic people – people who will challenge your thinking, be positive in times of high stress and anxiety, support and nurture your dreams, and enable you to achieve your goals. They also need to be honest with you, and be able to rein you in when you are in need of a gentle, or not so gentle, reminder.

Coaching sport is about motivating people. We are all in it for the same reason – to win. That means we all have to make those big calls. I wanted to be clear with every player about why they may have missed out on the team and what they could do to be in contention next time. I wanted to keep everyone in my squad as hungry and as competitive as possible. Brad Fleming was able to play in and win a World Cup in 2001 because he knew I still believed in him, despite the fact he missed out on the Commonwealth Games three years earlier. That was the kind of response to disappointment that I wanted to engender in my teams, and Warwick Talbut is the man who showed the way and has been a constant source of inspiration to me. Through him, I learned everything about team culture, and how to communicate effectively with my players. I also garnered a great deal of insight into how to seize opportunities and take leaps of faith. It was because of the way he treated people in business that I was able to understand my role in developing players for the professional game. Just as Warwick never wanted to stand in the way of someone's passion, I too knew that players would come and players would go on to other things.

It would have been easy to view this as a problem, and there would be times when I wished the pendulum sometimes swung the other way, but every time I saw a former New Zealand Sevens player shine in Super Rugby, or go on to fulfil a dream of playing for the All Blacks, I liked to think that a little bit of the time they had spent in our environment stayed with them. Better, I liked to think we'd helped them get to where they wanted to be.

Getting me to where I wanted to be in sevens required the assistance of many great people. When I first began coaching, I enlisted the help of Keith Roberts to develop a conditioning programme that would have my players fitter than anyone else. Keith was steeped in athletics training, and his intuition for conditioning and for a player's breaking point was second to none. Keith never once questioned my motives for working the guys as hard as I did. I knew he trusted me to know how far each and every one of them could go, and he never once lost his nerve in a training situation, or allowed a player to take the easy route. Fundamentally, he believed in me, and my programme, and that belief was enormously empowering when I was starting out as a coach. There would be many others who took up that role along the way. All of them were passionate about performance, and each sought new and innovative ways to whip players into the best possible shape. I was indebted to all of them, and to their dedication to the craft. I knew I had the right theories, but I needed specialists to really test them in real life.

Specialists like Jeni Pearce who revolutionised the way the team ate and how they thought about nutrition. Jeni truly was at the forefront of the sports nutrition movement in New Zealand, and her evangelical approach educated an entire generation of players on better eating habits. I may have been the one watching over them and sniffing out the fries, but it was Jeni's trained eye that set the wheels in motion for us. There have been many physiotherapists and doctors who have helped my guys be in optimum physical condition before and during tournaments as well. Kevin McQuoid was more than just a player panel-beater, however. He was a trusted confidant during tough selection decisions, and in his quiet, gentle and unassuming way, he could distil the mood of any team and counsel me on any issues that might arise. It was a fabulous skill of his and he was much sought after in professional rugby once he had finished his time with the New Zealand Sevens team.

I had superb managers, too. In the early days, they were appointed by the NZRFU for each and every tournament, but with the arrival of the professional game, Richard Crawshaw changed the management game forever, at least as far as I was concerned. Sadly, though his untimely death cut short his time with us, his tenure was the catalyst for me to ask for full-tenure managerial appointments to be made. That the annual award for the New Zealand Sevens Player of the Year is named in his honour is testament to the impact he made on us all. Ross Thurston, who filled those large shoes at the 1998 Commonwealth Games, and Tony Ward who would be with me for the Sevens World Cup victory and the first three years of the World Series, were meticulous men, highly organised and efficient, and trusted by the players and other members of the management team alike. Their patience and logistical ability were crucial during those massive years for the team.

There is one manager, however, who stands out. Ross Everiss had been my manager with the Bay of Plenty rugby team for several years when Tony Ward left the New Zealand Sevens team to take up a role with the Hurricanes. Rossco, as he was known to all, was a school teacher in Rotorua. He was an incredibly calm man with a great organisational touch and an easy rapport with the players. I sounded him out to see if he would be interested in the job with the New Zealand team and to my delight he answered in the affirmative. In December 2004, he came on board with the team, and was with me until the very last day of my tenure with New Zealand.

Not once did Rossco and I ever have an argument on tour because we were both keenly aware that players can sense any disagreement or division in a team. There were times when things weren't working the way I needed them to work, and those issues were always sorted with courageous conversations and swift action. There were certainly challenging times. A coach's role can be a lonely one in many ways, and you just need things to run as smoothly as possible. If there were issues around anything to do with the tournament, Ross would be charged with delivering that message. I'm sure the organisers thought I was an absolute pain in the arse, but I could be severely on edge as tournaments approached, and I had to have that trust in him that if circumstances were suboptimal, he would sort it out.

My manager was always the most important person in the team, the rudder by which the ship could sail straight. It didn't matter what they thought of what I wanted, they had to make it happen because they knew it was in the best interests of the team. I always wanted my team to be well prepared and to have everything they needed to perform. Whenever Ross, or Tony, or Craw was on the job, I knew it was always going to get done. They were my conduit to the tournament organisers and to the other members of the management team, and they were also the men I trusted to take our case to the NZRFU when I thought we needed support.

I was aware, always, of the need to be realistic in these situations and always tried to build a good argument first. If something is crucial to you, it is not hard to make a compelling case for it. 'Just because' is never enough, in any situation. Asking for resources or for funds has to come with the appropriate sales pitch and you can't pitch a half-baked idea. I tried to make sure I had all my ducks in a row when I sent Ross or any of the other managers into a situation where they would have to make a case on our behalf. Of course, my row of ducks didn't always line up as well as I would have liked!

───

With a fine management team in place, the New Zealand Sevens side reached all new levels of success. In 2000, 2001 and 2002, the team had each year been crowned World Series champions, winning 18 of the 30 tournaments played, including the World Cup in Argentina in 2001. We felt we were operating on a different level to the other sides, though none of us believed we could ever rest on our laurels. Part of the success came down to being able to develop specific game plans around the players we had. That was the joy of coaching sevens in many ways – you could design your plan around the players at your disposal.

As much as it was a joy, it was also a necessity. Because I had limited time to find players, and few places to find them, I would head into each year with no clear picture of who might put their hand up for selection. It taught me a valuable lesson in game design. If I had a couple of flyers in the backline – the likes of Jonah Lomu, Joeli Vidiri, Brad Fleming or Roger Randle – then we would develop a system to ensure we got the ball wide. In some teams, I may have pace across the board and be able to play a game of real speed that could fatigue any opponent. If I had an unbelievable five-eighth with a great step – the likes of Joe Tauiwi, Glen Osborne, Amasio Valence Raoma or Rua Tipoki – then I would need to hunt for a player who could operate as their foil on the field.

Most often, certainly in the professional fifteens game, you can design a plan and then select players to suit. That was rarely the case in sevens after the introduction of Super Rugby, and it forced me into fresh ways of thinking about the game. Sure, I had my wish list, but if a particular player was off limits to me, I would go back to the drawing board and start again. That's why my time in camp was so crucial to me. Apart from testing, it gave me a genuine sense of what I had at my disposal and how best I could utilise players' specific strengths for the betterment of the team. For example, over this period of time it became imperative to bring some real muscle to the breakdown, and we had a sensational array of young loose forwards who all were exceptional in the close-quarters battle. If ever we were having trouble dominating that part of the game, I would throw Chris Masoe or Rodney Soʻoialo into the mix, and more often than not the problem would be solved.

It was a period of regeneration for us. Our foundations – Dallas

Seymour and Eric Rush – would not be with us forever, and I needed to find players who could do the things they did. It was no easy task. Those two players were the very best in their roles over a long period of time, and everyone else who came after would be compared to them both on the field and off it. Still, the reality was that the game was getting faster, more physical and more youthful. I needed players to step up fast. In the first event of the 2002 season, Chris Masoe was a straight-up weapon for us. I had first come across him playing for Wanganui and it is fair to say he was not the most skilled player in terms of ball handling and vision. What he was, however, was dynamite in the post-tackle phase and he could genuinely hurt people in defence. That was his X-factor. When Chris got an understanding of the game, he just got better and better, and he gave everything he had on the field. He was the kind of player the Fijians used to loathe coming up against because he was so aggressive, and any player who could put a Fijian off his stride was worth having in your team.

Another player who was beginning to make a name for himself over this time was Hayden Reid. I will never forget him as long as I coach, because he was one of the most punishing trainers I had ever known. In the very first session I ever had him in camp, Hayden pushed himself so hard in the beep test that he had to go to hospital for a rehydration drip. I still remember walking into the ward and finding him there on the bed with a lure in his arm and a bag on a stand. I simply laughed at him.

'Hey Reido,' I said, between chuckles. 'Can you get out of here soon? I still need to see you play a game before I can pick you.'

I think he yanked the needle out of his arm and ran back to camp. He was a tough kid and a real workhorse on the field. With these kinds of players, we would go on to win the World Series that year, but we took a long time to get into the groove of the game. There was no doubt that other teams were fast catching on to the systems and processes we were using in training and game-play development, and Australia and South Africa in particular were growing into genuine contenders every tournament. They, like us, knew there was another special event that year and they were desperate to build some form. That was the 2002 Commonwealth Games in Manchester, and everyone wanted a shot at that medal.

We believed we had timed our run very well. After some mixed results at the beginning of the series, including another early exit at our home event in Wellington, we were able to win five of the last six World Series tournaments, only missing out on Hong Kong thanks to a three-point loss to our old Fijian rivals. From there we had conquered Singapore, Malaysia, England and Wales, and had a month back in New Zealand to settle on the side for Manchester. Once again, I was about to make one of the toughest decisions of my career.

Dallas Seymour had been back in the team for the last four wins of the World Series, and was still playing good sevens, if not great sevens by his lofty standards. Back in camp, I put the squad through its paces, desperately trying to gather all the data I needed to back my gut on what would be a very important team selection. When it came down to the crunch, Eric Rush would once again be captain, but his trusted lieutenant would not make the cut. Worse, I had to call Dallas on the phone rather than talk to him face to face. That was an incredibly heartbreaking phone call, and one I didn't want to make. It was especially hard for Dallas as his wife Julie had been picked for the Silver Ferns netball side, and I knew the two of them would have loved to have competed for New Zealand at the same Games, and potentially both win gold medals. I feared Dallas would have a real pop at me after I broke the news, but I should have known better. Clearly saddened, he nevertheless finished the call by asking me to pass on my best wishes to the team. That was the mark of the man, and he should be regarded always as one of our finest players.

We knew the Manchester Games would be very different to what we experienced in Kuala Lumpur, but the fact we had enjoyed medal success four years before, and had taken many key lessons from that event, gave us plenty of self-belief heading to England. I had made the decision to base ourselves away from the Games village before our tournament began, keen to avoid the distractions of other events at the village itself. Though not a popular decision in the eyes of some commentators, I was driven to give my team every chance to succeed, and keeping them relaxed and settled before the first match seemed to be a good idea. There was already enough planned as it was, including a trip to Manchester United's training base, where the boys were entertained by some of the biggest names in football. I, too, rubbed shoulders with coaching royalty, spending a good session chatting with Sir Alex Ferguson and comparing thoughts on fitness among other things.

Although I still felt for Dallas, I was supremely confident in the team I had picked to once again go for gold. We had brought back Bruce Reihana who had last played for the team in 1998, and he and Roger Randle gave us great pace and a good blend of vital experience. Eric Rush was there as always, in the engine room, supported by Chris Masoe and Rodney So'oialo, Craig Newby and Craig de Goldi. We had playmaking options in Amasio Valence

Raoma and Karl Tenana and the excitement of Brad Fleming, Anthony Tuitavake and Mils Muliaina. It had that balance I always looked for in a side, and a mean streak, too.

———

We certainly had no problems accounting for Canada, Niue and Scotland in pool play, although we had been scrappy in the second half against the Scots and we addressed that overnight ahead of the crunch games. Wales bore the brunt of that team talk in the quarterfinals and up next, in the semifinal, was Samoa, a team we had come to blows with earlier in the World Series, resulting in a number of suspensions. Worse, we had discovered a Samoan spy at our training run, too, which really pissed us off. Well and truly rarked up, we put 30 points on the Samoans and set up another Commonwealth Games final against Fiji. The game against Samoa did come at a cost, however. Eric had badly bruised his ribs, and would be unable to take the field in the final.

I was again forced to make a big selection call as we got ready to play for the gold medal. I could see that Anthony Tuitavake was in great form while Karl Tenana, my stand-in World Cup captain from the year before, was slightly off his game. I had to give the spot to Anthony, at Karl's expense and much to his chagrin. I remember Eric saying to me, 'Gee, Titch, I could never have made that call. Better you than me.' I knew what he meant, but I would have to live or die by that call. Anthony had none of Karl's experience, but I could tell he was good to go. I had to trust my instinct, as much as it was hard for Karl to take.

As it was, the boys that day had the measure of the Fijians once more. Though we trailed by one point in the second half, we kept our composure and kept the ball while all around us the Fijian players lost their heads, or tried to take ours off. They would finish the game with just five men on the park, and we would finish with two late tries to seal the deal. We were gold medallists again, in front of a sell-out crowd of close to 40,000 people. If feelings got any better, I sure hadn't experienced them yet. I was about to, though.

As we left the field following the medal ceremony, Eric Rush sidled up to me, carefully removed the medal from around his neck and placed it over my head. He had told me after the first victory in Kuala Lumpur that if he ever won another gold medal, he would give it to me. I never thought to take him seriously. Yet here I was, with the damn thing around my neck. I thought it was one of the most selfless acts of his selfless career. And I was grateful all over again that I had ever had the chance to call myself his coach.

12

DEPARTURES
AND
ARRIVALS

FREE OF THE rigours of fifteens coaching, I was loving every second of just being Gordon Tietjens, sevens coach. There was much to do every year in terms of planning and organisation, but the fact was that we were now in a rhythm of how the World Series and other pinnacle events fitted into each four-year cycle. And we were still winning. The 2002/03 series was our fourth consecutive series title and along the way we finally got to taste victory at our home tournament in Wellington. To win at home felt like a weight had been lifted off our shoulders, and it signalled the beginning of a fresh rivalry in the World Series, this time with a vastly improved England side. They had won the first tournament of the year in Australia and would also claim the Hong Kong title in the next tournament after Wellington. It was interesting to see how teams were starting to develop and I was keeping a close eye on how they were doing it.

I was also keeping a close eye on my own team. Eric had started the season as captain but I could tell, after 15 seasons of sevens, there was going to come a time when he simply wouldn't be able to keep up with the fitter, younger guys. He had character in spades, always had done, but there was little doubt sevens was becoming a young man's game, not just in New Zealand, but around the world.

I was rapt that he got the chance to lift the tournament trophy at home, especially after being injured at the 2001 World Cup, and for the 2002 Commonwealth Games gold medal match. If anyone deserved the adulation of his home fans it was that man.

While this book may be about my thoughts on coaching, culture, conditioning and leadership, many of the words could just as easily be Eric Rush's. He was always about the 'we' and never about the 'I'. He was prepared to work harder than the next guy for the opportunity to play, and when he played he would be the one who would make the massive tackles, who would chase every kick, who would get back up again and again to make the next play or to take the next pass. He was incredibly humble, passionate about the team, and adored by all the players who played for him. When I say played for him, I don't just mean in the traditional sense that he was their captain. They played for Eric because they believed in him.

When I had issues around selection or around player discipline, Eric would be the one to offer advice and wisdom. When we were scouting a team, or devising a plan of attack, Eric would know exactly what moves would work best in any situation. We were a team, he and I, and because of that, at the start of 2004 I picked up the phone and gave him a call.

'I can never drop you,' I told him. 'We've been through too much, and I respect you too much. You'll have to tell me when you've had enough. You'll have to be the one to make the call.'

I listened as there was a slight hesitation at the end of the line.

'Well then, Titch,' he said in his laconic way, 'I guess I'm done.'

Picking all along that this was the way he felt, I had one more trick up my sleeve for my old mate.

'Well, you can't this week because I need you in camp for Hong Kong and Singapore.'

So it was that Eric Rush made the last of his 62 tournament appearances for New Zealand. Alas, both were forgettable results, and he really deserved better than that. In Hong Kong we were knocked out of the semifinals by Argentina and a week later we were beaten in the plate final by Fiji. If there was one silver lining it was that Eric – Rushie – got one last try in his last game. Without Eric Rush, I don't know if New Zealand would have ever been quite the force that they became. His character shone through in everything the team achieved, and he should be held in the highest regard by any fan of sport in New Zealand. Captains like him are rare indeed, but he was every bit the leader that a Buck Shelford or Richie McCaw was. He just played sevens – and had better jokes.

With Eric's departure, the team felt like it had lost some of its swagger, although it kept producing the results that mattered in the World Series, claiming a fifth straight series crown in 2003/04. We still had talent coming through, though once again our selection pool was shrinking with the increased demands of expanded Super Rugby sides and precedence given to age-group representative sides – a decision that rankled me then and does still – and we continued to search high and low for players who could step into the system. We also needed a new breed of leaders, and a captain who could shoulder the burden.

Matua Parkinson and Liam Messam had shared the leadership in 2004; and in 2005, Liam, Orene Ai'i and Tafai Ioasa all had turns skippering the side. Despite each of them being fine players in their own right, the lack of one genuine leader was making life tough. We would still go on to comfortably win the World Series crown for a sixth time in 2005, but along the way we missed the chance to make it back-to-back World Cup victories. Instead, we were beaten and broken, left to watch a rapturous Fiji side take their victory lap in Hong Kong, much to the delight of the crowd. Though we bounced back the following week to once more claim the Singapore title, something was missing. That experienced, fun-filled core of the team no longer seemed to be there.

All up in that calendar year we used 30 players over just eight tournaments. In the last two tournaments of the series we were knocked out in the semifinals, first by South Africa, and then by France. I wondered if we had lost our magic or whether the constant chopping and changing, coming and going of personnel was just too much. We couldn't have unity in the team unless we were all in it together. I hoped that it was just a passing malaise, and that by the time we regrouped for the 2005/06 openers in Dubai and South Africa in December, we would be back on track, and ready to rediscover the team culture that had taken us so far for so long.

It was not to be the case. With a team of players returning from injury or absence, and some making their debuts, we were spat out in both the opening weekends of the series, and both times by Fiji in the cup quarterfinals. The Christmas break could not come quick enough. I was questioning my own role as coach, whether or not I had lost my knack for talent identification and for selection. I wondered if I had become too cute in what I was trying to do on the field, or if I had found the right guy to be my conduit to the team. I missed Eric Rush for a number of reasons, but probably more because he was a much older leader. I thought I knew how to deal with young athletes, was sure I was good at it, but I still harboured fears that perhaps my time had come and gone. I took a breather that summer, and took stock of where the team was at.

I still believed that sevens was all about the culture and conditioning that we had implemented when I first took over the team in 1994. Eleven seasons may have passed by, but that much had not changed. I had developed a wealth of knowledge – technical knowledge – on running lines and attack strategies and felt I was still passing on that information in an effective way. I had enlisted help on certain aspects of play in the hope that would lead to innovation and improvement in the team, and still believed we were consistent as a management group in how we treated everyone. We treated the players as individuals, but the team as one.

I thought, too, that I was playing to the strengths of my team. I had never been a spreadsheet coach and I had plenty of guys in the squad who had all the requisite versatility to be able to adapt to any game strategy. I also had Orene Ai'i and Amasio Valence Raoma, two men who could destroy any team when they expressed themselves. Did I have a point of difference, though? Every team needed one in the age of analysis. Perhaps we were just being shut down in our traditional areas of strength. Maybe the onus had to be on other members of the team to create chances, to mitigate that sort of coverage, and make an opponent second-guess their defensive strategy.

It was an intense few weeks of self-analysis, but I headed back to camp to prepare for the Wellington tournament intent on drilling down further into what had made us tick for the last 10 years. I wanted a team of workers, guys who would push each other incredibly hard at training and in the games, and know how to have fun after the hard yakka was over. We didn't have much time to rediscover our mojo. After Wellington and Los Angeles in

February of that year we would have just a month to prepare for the 2006 Commonwealth Games in Melbourne. It was amazing how quickly the last four years had gone, but that had become the norm in the demanding monthly grind of the World Series.

One player who I had started to notice was a young, humble loose forward from Counties Manukau called Derek Jamie 'DJ' Forbes. Forbes had first come to my attention at the National Sevens, which thankfully had been moved to January to give us the opportunity to look at talent before we made the final contracting decisions of the year, and before the home tournament in Wellington. He was a tireless worker who seemed to hunt down ball carriers from anywhere on the park. He rarely died in the tackle when he had the ball himself, and the number of turnovers he could win in a game was astonishing. At the beginning of 2006, he was in the New Zealand squad, but by the end of the year (the start of the new season's World Series) he would be captaining the side.

He reminded me so much of Dallas Seymour, the way he gritted his teeth in training and just worked his arse off all the time. Off the field, he was incredibly polite and humble with a deep religious faith, but put him on the field and he could boss a game, talking to team-mates, communicating with his link players, and generally causing havoc at the breakdown. I didn't know it at the time, but DJ would go on to become the most-capped player in World Series history. If I had been fretting over the previous summer about finding a leader to replace the irreplaceable Eric Rush, by the end of 2006 my search was over. DJ would be my captain for the next 10 seasons and he would invariably be the hardest-working man in the game. He was Rushie Mk II – just without the sweet tooth.

___

That was all in the near future, however. My immediate future as coach was not looking altogether rosy. I had thought that the break might do the team good, that we would all have a chance to decompress, and then get back to basics in the first training camp of the new season. There were positive signs, but still there was something missing – that magic spark that all great teams need. I was still struggling to put my finger on the root cause of the problem, and further introspection was getting me nowhere. I went back to old faithful, and we trained hard heading into Wellington. It was all to no avail. Yet again, we were defeated by our old foes Fiji, in the cup semifinals. It was a galling loss in front of our home fans who we always wanted to win for. A week later we suffered the same fate at the hands of the same team in Los Angeles. Once more, I turned inward to search for answers. The truth was that we were playing a brutalist style of sevens, built around possession and power at the breakdown. It was the best way to make use of the players we had.

Perhaps, I thought, we could bring in some extras who just may be able to bring a bit more to the role. It was a little against the grain to find players to suit a plan, rather than the other way around, but with players released from Super Rugby contracts for the games, I took my opportunity. Liam Messam, Josh Blackie and Tanerau Latimer came into the side to bolster the forwards, and Sosene Anesi and Tamati Ellison were selected to give us some gas. It was Melbourne or bust. One last chance to turn around our season.

I was not overly confident after our first day of action at Melbourne's Telstra Dome. Unlike Manchester where the sevens had been held on the last couple of days of competition, in Melbourne we were the first cab off the rank. We had prepared as best we could, only losing Doug Howlett to injury in the lead-up, but we were still sluggish on the opening day, taking down Wales, Namibia and Kenya with scorelines that rather flattered us. We knew, too, after getting out of our pool section, that we were on a collision course with the home side in the semifinals. Perhaps with our minds on that task we were once again not quite the real deal against Canada in the quarters.

Still, a win was a win, and with Rushie beside me, this time as an assistant coach, we prepared the guys for what they were about to face. It was a big crowd in Melbourne, in a genuine stadium that was as colourful as it was noisy. Our guys were accustomed to big crowds, but this one would be particularly parochial. To this day, I don't know how, but we got through that match by the skin of our teeth. Amasio Valence Raoma and Cory Jane were the saviours on the scoresheet, but it was the work of players like Josh Blackie, Lote Raikabula and Liam Messam that really set the tone for what was to come.

Everyone was expecting Fiji to beat England in their own semifinal, but England, coached by Mike Friday and captained by Simon Amor who in turn would go on to coach the side, were too clever for the Fijians. Suddenly we had a very different challenge in front of us. England were fast, well organised and well coached. We had to be on top of our game. From the opening whistle in that final, we certainly were. I had not seen this level of performance in months. Josh Blackie was a man possessed. A gnarly and rangy loose forward, he bestrode the Melbourne turf like a colossus. Everywhere I looked in the opening spell, Josh was hunting ball runners or in great support space.

Cory Jane opened the scoring off a scrum before England hit back to level the scores midway through the first spell. It was the kick we needed and Amasio sprang to life, pulling rabbits out of hats at every turn. He set Josh up for a second, and then helped Lote Raikabula into space for a third. We were 15–7 up at the break and feeling like we were in control. Of course, that's exactly when the game of sevens bites you.

England were first to score after the break and the game was finely balanced – a one-point lead was all we had. I needed the guys to stay calm and trust in the plan. We had looked to play with extra width, in an attempt to tire out the English defence. We knew they thought we would keep it tight, but Amasio had the ball on a string and a licence to run the show. Soon enough, he set up Liam Messam for a fourth try, and then Josh was over once again, running on the angle and busting tackles to score. We had a 15-point lead with three minutes to go, and then we tackled England out of the game.

The full-time horn was the sweetest sound in the world. We were Commonwealth Games champions for the third straight time. How we had managed such a turnaround after the last few months was beyond me. Well, almost. We were the fittest team on the park. That was our point of difference. The old methods had worked once again.

———

It would be nice to think that they would continue to work that season, but if results are anything to go by, that would not be the case. After the elation of Melbourne, we were back to the reality of a pick-and-mix team for the remainder of the 2005/06 season. I realised very quickly that we had bottled the lightning for that magical moment in Melbourne and we were unable to take the lid off. We tried our best but the likes of Liam Messam and Josh

Blackie were back to fifteens and Amasio Valence Raoma would call time on his sevens career – a great sevens career at that. We missed his playmaking genius greatly, and the season concluded with a very disappointing fourth-place finish.

I was downcast because the World Series was our bread and butter. We simply had to find a way to be a threat in each and every tournament, instead of being an easy mark for a semifinal exit. I needed to go out and find players again. The hunt, it seemed, was never going to be over for me. I had a framework of a team, an outline that I needed to fill in. The 2005/06 series had reminded me of what I had set out to achieve when I took on this job. I wanted to have that great team unity again, to find committed players who could deliver every time they took the field. I had good players in the squad, make no mistake, but the sum was not greater than the total of its parts.

A year later, that feeling would be very different. With DJ leading the way, we once again managed to claim the Sevens World Series in what was to be the start of another special era of sevens. We ushered in some new names, clearing the decks and looking for a team that could perform consistently throughout the series. DJ was joined by Solomon King and Zar Lawrence and Ed Cocker, who had been spotted playing for the Otago Barbarians side at nationals. All three of them would go on to play a big part in the team's fortunes. There were players like Nigel Hunt and Afeleki Pelenise, Nick Thomson and Willie Rickards. They were anything but household names, but they had humility, respect, a work ethic and a sense of purpose. When you have those things, you have enough.

That side got New Zealand back into a winning habit. They were a great bunch of boys to be around and they worked enormously hard for each other, both around the training field and in games. It didn't always come easy for them either. Remarkably, after victory in South Africa, that team was knocked out by Fiji in the next four cup semifinals, in Wellington, San Diego, Hong Kong and Adelaide. They never once dropped their heads or pointed the finger at one another. They simply came back to camp, worked harder than ever, and set their minds to doing better in the next event.

It will go down in history as perhaps the greatest series win since the first in 1999. After defeating Fiji in the cup final in the penultimate tournament in England, the boys were still 10 points adrift of their rivals in series standings going into Edinburgh. If Fiji made it to the semifinals, the crown was theirs for the second consecutive year. In a twist of fate that still makes me shake my head to this day, Wales sent Fiji packing in the quarterfinals. Led by a two-try effort from DJ Forbes, New Zealand duly beat Samoa in the final, and scooped the prizes in one of the more amazing days of my coaching tenure.

––––––

Something else had happened in 2008 that had given me newfound confidence in the balance of the team. We had unleashed as our playmaker a diminutive Fijian by the name of Tomasi Cama. Tomasi was every ounce the playmaker that Amasio Valence Raoma and Joe Tauiwi had been, but with the added bonus (from some people's point of view) of being the most wildly unpredictable player I think I have ever selected. I knew he was going to be in for the long haul. All the team needed now was a couple of finishing touches. As I had found out so many times before, you never know when or where you are going to find the next great player. It just so happened that he was at a club tournament, playing for Hinuera, in Te Awamutu.

Unlike in fifteens, where talent is placed on a professional conveyor belt at a very young age, sevens has never been about ready-made athletes at the highest level. Sure, back in 1994 I inherited some of the finest players in the country, players who could be conditioned for the game, but as rugby changed due to professionalism and the advent of Super franchises, I was having to dig deeper than ever before to unearth the next player who could give me something special on a sevens field. Playmakers were the toughest guys to find. It is a position that has so much importance in the game of sevens. Joe Tauiwi was the very first and delivered at both the provincial and the international level. Joe was someone who had all the natural ability and, once he had a sniff, he trained the house down. Joe was a Ngongotaha boy and ultimately kept All Black halfback Graeme Bachop out of the starting side in 1994. After Joe, there had been Amasio Valence Raoma, a kid spotted in a pick-up game against New Zealand Fijians. He was a schoolboy, yet he had the desire to train and the vision to play and he went on to have a fabulous career. There were guys like Glen Osborne and Karl Tenana who could both make magic on the field. They came from small towns, tiny clubs, schoolyards. They were out there, I just had to find them before someone else did.

I would look at a game of fifteens and spot mobile locks and fast loose forwards. I would look for any back with genuine pace, or a special step or an ability to swerve and weave through a defensive line. I would look for halfbacks with outstanding hand–eye coordination, or a willingness to run. Augustine Pulu was that kind of halfback, and he would later go on to become an Olympian.

As I had found out so
many times before,
you never know
when or where you
are going to find the
next great player.

Troy Flavell was a guy who didn't have the skills for sevens in terms of his ball work, but boy could he hurt players in defence. He was a forerunner of the likes of Josh Blackie and Liam Messam. In short, I was looking for anyone and anything that could help my team in a game of sevens. I could always pick a player on instinct and trust myself to give him the right coaching and conditioning to become everything I thought he could be. It doesn't always happen that way, but when it does it's a wonderful thing.

I was thinking about all that standing there on the sideline watching that club sevens tournament in Te Awamutu. I was thinking about that because I couldn't take my eyes off a tall, skinny white kid who was running rings around everyone. After the game, I wandered over to him and asked what position he played. In his quiet voice, he told me that he played either fullback or first five. I laughed at that, having thought he was a tall loose forward when I watched him play. I suspect I was already thinking about what position I would play him at. I told him that I'd like to invite him to a camp in Mount Maunganui the following weekend and asked him if he was available. He nodded, said nothing more, and we left it at that.

The next week the squad got its very first look at Tim Mikkelson. He wandered – sauntered – into the camp looking like he had spent the intervening days in a hippie commune. He was most definitely a different kind of character – as relaxed as if he had been born in a vaporiser, he was in shorts and jandals and looked like he couldn't give a damn about being in the camp, or about what we might have in store for him. The other players were staring at this interloper thinking I had lost my mind! Even Rossco, who knows better than most not to judge a book by its cover, looked at me sideways.

'What the hell are you doing with this guy, Titch?' he asked.

I laughed at that. I just looked at him as if to say, 'Trust me', and we hit the gymnasium to put the boys through their beep test. Needless to say, Tim won the test, with some ease. Then he went out onto the field and smashed everyone in 150-metre sprints. Then he smoked them in the shuttles. It was fair to say that no one looked sideways at Tim in our camp ever again. He was the real deal.

The only problem Tim had was that he was the quietest man I had ever met. I mean, he did not say a word. Ever. I remember saying to him as the new season rolled around at the end of 2006, 'I can't pick you, Tim, unless you are actually going to say something on the field.' Imagine someone telling you that you couldn't play because you're a mute! It had to be that way, though. Communication was a fundamental skill for me. In big stadia with noisy crowds, you have to be able to make yourself heard.

There was only one problem after that. I could never shut him up again. The more confident he became in that environment, the louder he got. I should be pleased, really. With his first touch in his first World Series tournament he set up a try with a 70-metre run and has never looked back. In fact, he has gone on to become one of the greatest sevens players of all time. Not bad for a skinny white boy running around for a country team on a dusty field in the middle of the Waikato hinterland.

13

AN
AWAKENING

IF EVER I went to a tournament and came away with one or two names that I could invite to a training camp, I was over the moon. It seemed like I was always on a treasure hunt, following tips from coaches, heading to club tournaments or provincial camps, receiving reports from scouts. Always, there were names, dates, games. I never wanted to stop discovering talent; never once thought I could rest on my laurels. The World Series was attritional, and back-up was always required to cover injuries or to replace players who left the programme for the chance to play fifteens.

Over the years, I had always trusted my instinct for a player's natural ability. I had trained my eye to spot that one thing that I could harness to transform a player from promising to professional. So many had already been found, but I was never satisfied and would continue to seek new faces as long as I coached the game. It was certainly getting harder and I thought that was a shame. It was never going to be possible to latch on to a player like Christian Cullen again. I just wouldn't have a chance to bring him into sevens before the fifteens system had him locked away. I'm sure Christian would have gone on to superstardom without sevens, but I still believe that exposing him early to those levels of training and that big global audience in Hong Kong was an important step in his career. I was thrilled that I'd had the chance to work with him but was somewhat disappointed that, well after I was gone, the next generation of New Zealand Sevens coaches may never get such an opportunity to spot and select a talent like him again.

I had always believed that succession was the secret. It was challenging in an era of high player turnover, but that was the reality of the situation and there was little point complaining. Things were not going to change in terms of New Zealand rugby's preference for the fifteens game, and so it was imperative that we just worked harder to bring through new faces. It was all about creating and sustaining the perfectly balanced side, one that was built upon three pillars: experience, performance and enthusiasm.

Sometimes you had to be tough on those players once you found them and got them into camp. Even the most talented kids can fail to achieve selection if their work ethic is found wanting. There really was only one Jonah Lomu in my time, a man whose incredible skill set trumped his struggles on the training field. He was something special, and I knew with him that once he got into a game, there was no way he would let either me or his captain down. There may be a lot of kids who think they are Jonah, but I can assure you, and them, that they are not.

Israel Dagg was once a player who relied a lot on his natural talent. I remember Izzy coming into the team as a youngster, but for all the hype around him he just didn't seem to have the will to dig in and get the work done in camp. Midway through the 2008 season, despite the fact we had started the series on an absolute tear, I had to get him motivated to work harder. I thought long and hard about it and eventually drove to Hawke's Bay to have a conversation with him. He was not going to be part of the team going to Hong Kong that year. He still to this day says that was a

Jonah was something special, and I knew with him that once he got into a game, there was no way he would let either me or his captain down.

massive wake-up call for him – he had never before been dropped from any team and he was frankly stunned that I would drive all that way to tell him why. He wasn't performing as well as I knew he could and he needed to be fitter. I wanted to make sure that was a positive message for him, which is why I was keen to deliver it face to face. After that, he never had an issue with fitness in my team again, and would come back and be a part of what was a very successful squad.

With many players, I can see immediately that they have significant value based on their work rate alone. These are the players who can push when it really hurts. I knew if I had guys who were willing to do the extras, they would win tournaments for me. I often thought back to my early years with the team and well remember Eric Rush getting the boys up on cold mornings in Palmerston North to have a run before breakfast. Then they would train all morning and do it all over again in the afternoon. It was all team-driven, and it was rewarding as a coach to see that.

New Zealand rarely had the fastest players in the world game, but it was rare that we didn't have the hardest-working players. That's what you have to demand from any team, in business as well. If you see someone turning up day after day, putting in the hours in order to get the results, that person should be rewarded for their effort. I tried to reward the players who were prepared to go to the wall for me. In 2007 and 2008, I had those players, and they were about to do something no New Zealand team had ever achieved.

I had come to have a strange coaching superstition after all those years in charge of the team. I don't know when I first thought about it, or how it developed, but usually I could get a sense of how well the side would go in any given tournament by how the environment felt after the last training of the assembly week. The mood would tell me everything I needed to know about how the boys were mentally. If they were in great spirits, cracking jokes and taking the piss out of each other, I felt that they were in the right space. It was the old theory: do the work, then have the fun.

If training had been particularly messy or there were some concerns about getting things right, or a lack of self-belief within the team, that laughter would be missing. Those were the times I worried about how well we would perform in the upcoming matches. It was a laugh-o-meter reading of the mood of the team, and it told me so much about how well we were prepared for the weekend, and how confident the guys were in their ability to go the distance. Though rather unscientific, I always listened for the laughter after that final session, and it was, believe it or not, incredibly accurate.

It had been missing for much of the previous season. The player changes and constant reshuffling of the deck had been a burden on the side, and the disruptions were not conducive to great team unity – something that every sevens side needed in order to thrive. This year, I could tell the spirit was back. It was an awakening of spirit the likes of which I had not seen for some time. It wasn't just the players either. I felt alive in the environment as well. We had balance, confidence, great playmaking ability in Tomasi Cama, and a team that rolled up its sleeves and went to work. It was the beginning of a run like none before.

It had started back in May of 2007 when the team clicked into gear in the final two tournaments of the season. In doing so, they had won the World Series after what had been a season of mixed results.

There had been the Commonwealth Games gold medal the year before, but not much to celebrate since. With wins over Fiji and Samoa in England and Scotland respectively, the team had found its fire again, and by the start of the new season in December, that fire was absolutely raging.

It was a team of grafters, really; men who would go out and work themselves so hard no team could withstand the pressure. The likes of Ed Cocker and Steven Yates, Zar Lawrence and Solomon King, Nigel Hunt and Victor Vito were not household names in New Zealand rugby, but put them in a sevens jersey and they were absolutely extraordinary. Israel Dagg was going to be a special player, of that everyone was certain, while Rene Ranger would rampage his way into All Blacks contention a few years later – along with Victor and Israel. Tim Mikkelson would take his first tentative steps to becoming a sevens legend over this period, and the mainstays of Cama, Raikabula and Forbes were the Tauiwi/Rush/Seymour combination reborn.

In Wellington in February they picked up exactly where they had left off, and Victor Vito thrilled his home fans with a two-try effort in the final against Samoa, the last of which would be a siren-beating match-winner. I well remember the stadium in the capital that evening. It was the Wellington Sevens at its very best and one of the most electric crowds I had ever experienced. When Vic scored that winning try, I thought the place was going to tear itself apart, and I don't know if I have ever seen a New Zealand team beaming so brightly after a World Series win.

In San Diego a week later, they were at it again. In the first four games of that tournament, including a quarterfinal against Fiji, the team conceded just one try. They conceded just five in total across the six games played, which included a 27–12 win over the South

Africans in the final. It was a victory that had all the hallmarks of the great New Zealand wins. It was built upon character and pride, as defence always is. In Hong Kong the following month, they repeated the dose. Again they conceded just five tries in the tournament and, again, it was South Africa on the receiving end of a 26–12 scoreline in the final.

I put so much of the success of this period down to the follow-me leadership of DJ Forbes. He never complained about training hard, always demanded excellence from those around him, and was an expert communicator on the field with a great feel for the game and the ability to work many moves ahead of the opposition. There were no histrionics, just calm and thoughtful leadership and an enormous amount of self-discipline that meant he was always in the best shape he could be. He had filled the void created by Eric Rush's departure, and the team responded to his warmth and honesty.

After Hong Kong, it was on to Adelaide for the Australian leg, where defensively the boys couldn't sustain their high standards. Although they made it through to the cup final, South Africa would finally get one over them and hand them their first defeat in 11 months. All up, that team won seven consecutive tournaments, completing an unbeaten run of 47 games. It bettered the previous New Zealand record of six tournaments and 40 games set in 2001/02. Though there was disappointment at the loss, I impressed upon DJ and the team that what they had done over the previous 11 months was nothing short of extraordinary.

Though the run was over, the achievement was real and valuable. The team would only miss one final in the entire season, which would be in the next event in England where they were knocked out by the hosts in the quarters, but what pleased me most was that the following week they put it all behind them and won the final event of the season in Scotland. There was no finger-pointing after England, no blame laid at the feet of any individual. They just got back into their work and found the resolve to finish on a high note. To me, that said everything about the character of that team. It was small on stars, but huge on hard work.

It is funny to think that among all the titles and the medals our teams won, that team still stands out for me. Even in the days when I had Jonah Lomu, Christian Cullen and the big names of the day, one thing we always realised was that no star was ever bigger than the team. Without the guys there to make the tackles and the turnovers, or to make the breaks, the others would never have been able to function or to shine. The guys in that 2007/08 side stood out to me because they pushed each other mercilessly at training and all worked as equals in games. The starting seven at that stage was so unbelievably fit as a result that they could have played every minute of every game. When you have a backbone like that, anything is possible.

Nothing lasts forever in this game and the following year proved much tougher, as did the year after that. It was clear that our dominance in 2008 had sparked the other programmes to life. South Africa began to throw valuable resources at the game, understanding that their talent pool in terms of speed was probably second to none in the world game. They would win their first World Series in 2009, and the following year the Samoans, based on pure athleticism and superior vision for the game, would claim a maiden title. Throwing a spanner in the works in 2009 was the fact that Wales managed to win the World Cup. It was the most surprising result in the history of the event and it certainly made the traditional powerhouse teams stand up and take notice, ourselves included.

Watching and analysing competitors became more important than ever before. I knew that in business it was crucial to understand where your competitors were at, what strengths they had and what opportunities they were going after. The more you could learn about them, the better placed you would be to get the jump on them and to win clients that may have been theirs for years. Of course, in business, you could always make an offer for your competitor's best staff to join you. That unfortunately was not the case with coaching a national side.

What we did do was thoroughly review why we weren't able to win games, or why teams like South Africa and Samoa, and many others who were improving every year, were enjoying success. We wanted an intimate knowledge of all the key threats each team possessed. It was about patience, understanding how the game dynamic changed with substitutions, or if a team had a couple of key players out with injury. Teams were certainly doing the same analysis on us and we needed to be more aware of how to strike and at what times to do it.

In the main, we needed to treat every game like a final because we knew every side wanted desperately to beat us. We were the team that had won more series titles than any other, and as such a win over us was seen as a massive boost to other teams. We wore that as a badge of honour. It was representative of a standard we had set long ago and one which we were desperate to maintain. We relished the challenge, but not always the one familiar tactic most often employed against us. What many teams tried to do when

We needed to treat every game like a final because we knew every side wanted desperately to beat us.

they played us was slow the game down. They understood that they would be unable to stay with us if they were forced to play at our speed. We wanted to play fast and loose on attack, working hard for turnovers and launching counterattack plays. Other teams would rather force the game to set piece off lineouts and control the tempo through regular stoppages. It was very frustrating at times, and we were constantly searching for ways to mitigate that style.

We wanted to always dominate possession, and more often than not at halftime that was the message to the players. Although I would look animated, my talk was always as concise, clear and simple as I could make it. I was always aware of how fatigued players are during the breaks between halves, especially on the second day of a tournament when they are five, sometimes six, games into the schedule. That imperative to keep the ball and play with speed was another reason fitness always had to be the primary focus. There were countless times when we had been able to win games after the final siren because we were fit enough to keep playing until the other team finally relented. We had seen it with Victor Vito in Wellington and we would see it again in the biggest game of 2010 – the Commonwealth Games final in Delhi.

———

The selection of the Commonwealth Games team always became a very stressful time for me. It was a four-yearly event, had enormous significance to the general sporting public in New Zealand – sadly for the players, much more than the World Series or Sevens World Cup – and always involved a sudden injection of fifteens players who often, through sheer talent and the ability to condition themselves quickly to the sevens game, would take the place of a player who had busted his hump for me during tournaments throughout the season.

It had taken on an even greater significance for the fact that in October 2009 the International Olympic Committee had accepted sevens into the Olympic Games for 2016. It was a massive moment for the sport and it was wonderful to see Jonah Lomu in the thick of it, having been a key spokesperson for the campaign to give sevens its Olympic shot. I wanted the Commonwealth Games process to be my guide on how the Olympics would work, and that added another layer of complexity to what was already a complicated selection strategy.

DJ Forbes would be captain of the side and he would be joined by the core of our series team: Tim Mikkelson, Lote Raikabula and Tomasi Cama. Having those four men at the heart of the plan allowed me to blend pace and strength around them. Sherwin Stowers, Hosea Gear, Kurt Baker and Zac Guildford offered plenty of pace, while the strength came from Liam Messam and Ben Souness, a young Taranaki forward who had been one of the players of the tournament at that year's national championships in Queenstown. Rounding out the team was Toby Arnold, a Bay of Plenty utility with a massive ticker who offered great service as a staunch defender and linkman.

Liam's inclusion was vital, for only he and Lote had been to the Commonwealth Games before. It made me realise just how quickly I had churned through players in the intervening years, how many had come and gone through the system and often on to high-profile places in the professional fifteens game. I didn't dwell long on that fact – instead I was determined to make sure we made it four gold medals in a row. The expectation of the public was one thing, but it was nothing compared with the expectation of the team.

On 12 October 2010, in the fading light of a dusky Delhi afternoon, that expectation became reality when Kurt Baker took an inside ball from Sherwin Stowers and scored the match-winning try against Australia in the final. It had been an epic contest, one in which we had trailed the Australians for much of the game. At halftime, I had simply told the boys that they were fitter, and that if they kept the ball, they would break their opposition. It was obvious that as the second half unfolded they were beyond fatigue. First Sherwin scored, then DJ Forbes. Suddenly a 7–17 deficit had been turned into a 19–17 lead. With three minutes remaining, Kurt and Sherwin set up the crucial break from deep in their own 22 and sealed the game 24–17.

Kurt was the kind of kid to give aspirin a headache and was undoubtedly the biggest pest in the team. The fact that he started to celebrate before he put the ball down almost ended me that day. But he finally scored, I leapt in the air and started running around in circles, and the boys closed out the match for another memorable win. It was the fourth straight Commonwealth Games medal for New Zealand. After the challenges of the last two World Series results, it felt like everything was back on track. Order had been restored.

14

DELIVERING
THE GOODS

THE COMMONWEALTH GAMES victory in Delhi would be the start of a magical run for the team. New Zealand rugby in general would enjoy a golden age, with the All Blacks winning their home World Cup in 2011, ending a title drought of 24 years and going a long way to erase the pain of previous World Cup losses. There was a sense that rugby had recaptured a jaded market, and I felt we were in good shape in the sevens programme to snare some of that newfound zest for the game. I redoubled my efforts in player identification but now, more than ever, I was searching for players who genuinely wanted to give sevens their all.

We still didn't have a contracting system that allowed fully for development, but we made the best of the situation. We had our tier-one players – those who were solely focused on sevens – which gave us some certainty for most of the season, albeit with the ever-present risk of injury to deal with. We also had players on tier-two and -three contracts, which gave them some flexibility around playing both sevens and fifteens. It wasn't always ideal, with Super Rugby squads ever-hungry to vacuum up youngsters to cover trainings and to become acclimatised to their own strength and conditioning programmes. They were antithetical approaches. I wanted leaner and faster men, whereas Super Rugby's premium on contact required bigger and stronger athletes.

We made it function as well as we could, and because it kept producing results, no thought was given to how the system could better accommodate sevens as a concurrent sport to fifteens. All coaches were naturally selfish when it came to their own requirements, and I was no exception. Still, I couldn't help wondering after all these years why so many coaches saw sevens less as a legitimate sport and a genuine pathway, and more as a jolly to be played in front of crowds of expat punters. I knew that sevens worked as a development sport for fifteens talent, as much as it survived as its own standalone game. While it required a specialist fitness, it was still fundamentally about running, tackling, passing and catching. Those were transferable skills, as any number of All Blacks who had started their careers as sevens players could attest. Contract issues aside, I wanted guys to give sevens a shot. I knew it worked for them, I knew it would be better for their careers than holding tackle bags all season in Dunedin or Wellington, and I knew what I was looking for. All I needed to know was that the players themselves were looking for the same thing.

Over the next several years, I made a point of making sure any player I was interested in bringing into the camp truly wanted to be there. We had worked so hard to rediscover team harmony, and to find that unity that we had first enjoyed back when I began in 1994. I didn't want to jeopardise that by bringing in players who weren't that interested in making a go of it, or who didn't have the drive to make their time with us count. You can't afford to have people like that in any organisation. Either they are 100 per cent in or they had better be 100 per cent out. I had lived that philosophy during my time as coach. I was fully invested in the sevens programme when we were in camp or away on tournament duty and, each

Monday when I arrived home, I would be in my car and back to the office to make sure everything was in order in my day job at Bay Engineers. If I could have the energy to care deeply about both roles, then any player I had could at least care deeply about the New Zealand Sevens team.

Yes, occasionally they would crack under pressure. That was what the training was designed to do. That's why it was supposed to be harder than any game the guys would play. If they could withstand that, they could withstand anything a tournament had to throw at them. Even the great players had sooner or later lost it on the training paddock. I well remember Karl Tenana in Hong Kong years before, flying off the handle after the team was given another session of shuttle runs to complete. I took great delight in cracking guys like Karl. It made them stronger mentally, and Karl went on to become one of the very best in the world, after rediscovering his sense of humour.

Yes, sevens had a reputation for the rigorous nature of its training and testing regime. Well, in my mind that was a good thing. If you wanted to be a professional rugby player, surely benchmarking yourself in that kind of environment was a good place to start. If nothing else, you would quickly discover where you were really at. Though my theories on training may have seemed outdated to some, the All Blacks were happy for me to take a few sessions with the backs and the loose forwards in the lead-up to the Rugby World Cup, and along with Nic Gill, the All Blacks' head of strength and conditioning, I was also tasked with putting halfback Piri Weepu through his paces ahead of the tournament.

That felt like a legitimisation of my work, and I was only too happy to help. However, not everyone was so convinced of my training methods, or my sport, for that matter. Over the first decade of the twenty-first century, the player agency business had also grown exponentially. In and of itself, that was understandable, not to mention beneficial to the players they represented. It did mean that there was another filter to go through as a coach. I used to deal directly with the player, then deal through the union, but now the agents were the all-important factor in the mix. You had to know who those agents were and what their players were up to. It was not surprising that they saw Super Rugby or offshore contracts as more valuable than a deal in sevens. While sevens had some profile, especially during the Wellington and Commonwealth Games tournaments, it was an undeniable fact that the coverage our players received was nowhere near what Super Rugby and All Blacks players did. Every kid wants to be noticed, and rugby players are no exception. In my opinion, there was a disconnect between the achievements of my players and the profile they enjoyed – one that compounded the issues around selection and commitment.

My overriding concern was that potential players were getting the wrong advice. Who were they listening to? And what were they being told about what sevens would do for them or mean for their career? In my time as New Zealand coach, I had seen so many young guys come through the sevens programme and move on to sustained success in fifteens. Many of them had also got the chance to represent their country at the Commonwealth Games, and soon they could also have the chance to become Olympians. I would always stress that a gold medal means an awful lot to the players who have won one, and the one tucked away in my drawer means even more to me.

There was one player during this time who exemplified the kind of commitment I was looking for. I watched him playing for Taranaki, a fresh-faced farm kid straight out of high school, at the National Sevens in Queenstown, and instantly admired what I saw. For one so young, he was a visionary player – composed, fast, brave in the tackle, and superbly fit. Afterwards I asked him if he would be interested in attending a training camp with the team, and his eyes lit up. He was happy to take up the offer and shook my hand so hard he nearly broke it. Whenever he reported for duty afterwards, I knew I was at risk of fractured fingers. He was such a down-to-earth, humble guy, and he came to every training camp that season. I was always tempted to pick him, but with more experienced guys in the team I thought it better that he should find his feet in the environment and work hard at his game understanding and conditioning. He finally got his chance on the final leg of the World Series, in England and Scotland, and I knew he would be ready to feature heavily the following season.

Unfortunately, I wouldn't get the chance to pick Beauden Barrett again. He was selected for the Hurricanes the following year after a breakthrough season with the Taranaki provincial side, and that was that as far as his time in sevens went. I certainly hoped at the time that I would see him again one day, but he had other things to achieve first. In 2015, he would win a Rugby World Cup with the All Blacks, and the following year he would receive the honour of being named World Rugby Men's Player of the Year. I was thrilled that he'd at least had a chance to play sevens for his country.

There were others who would pop up in the unlikeliest of places. Declan O'Donnell was playing a club tournament for Waikato side Te Rapa when I first laid eyes on him. It was the only thing anyone could lay on him that day, for the defence couldn't touch him.

He was a wonderfully balanced player, with dancing feet and a big engine. His younger brother Kylem would also join the side soon after him and together they were a lethal combination. Joe Webber also burst onto the scene around the same time. Again, he was just playing a club tournament in the Waikato, but he was playing on another planet compared with everyone else on show, stepping through entire teams and running in 90-metre tries. I knew nothing about him the first time I saw him play – had never even heard his name before. After I had watched his game, I found out he had been in the Waikato age-group sides, but the only side I wanted him in was mine.

All four of those players had that one special thing in their game that I knew I could build on. They were also hungry for a chance, knew exactly what they wanted, and what the opportunity meant to them. That sense of purpose is a prerequisite for success. If a player doesn't possess that desire, then no amount of coaching or cajoling is ever going to help them be all they can be. Guys like Beauden, Joe, Declan and Kylem all knew that the sevens pathway was right for them at the time, and they were busting down the door to join up.

———

It is important to note that there were players through the years who had outrageous skill sets yet who were never selected to train with the squad or play with the team. If much of my eye for talent was based on instinct, there was a fair amount based on first impressions, too. I always wanted to meet new players and talk with them first, rather than simply expressing an interest in their services through their unions or managers. That first face-to-face meeting could tell me everything I needed to know about how much desire a kid had. If their response to the offer of being part of the squad was equivocal, I would often simply move on.

To me, every day is a job interview. I was convinced that these kids – many of whom were fresh out of age-group teams and taking their first tentative steps into a professional sporting career – would, if nothing else, benefit from exposure to high-intensity training in a representative environment. If they couldn't recognise the opportunity that was being offered to them, I didn't see the need to spell it out further. Often, I could sense that they were in two minds because they were holding out for a Super Rugby contract. A bird in the hand is worth two in the bush, as the saying goes. They could grab and go, or they could wait and wish.

It was usually a one-chance policy. If I couldn't get in touch with the player, or thought there was a prospect I hadn't yet met out there who might have something to offer, I would sometimes go through the agents, too. I never wanted to be seen to be chasing a player more than was necessary. I was all too aware that my interest could be used as a bargaining tool with Super Rugby coaches and had no interest in being a pawn in that game. I was not there to help prop up a player's contract value. More than that, I was of the fervent and quite legitimate belief that I shouldn't have to convince anyone that playing for their national side was a good idea. If they needed convincing of that, then they weren't fit for the position in the first place.

When you have a team of players who believe in what they are doing and who cherish the jersey, the humility and respect shines through in all they do. I was proud of the victories we achieved, but I was equally proud of the fact that there had never been a superstar syndrome in our programme. Everyone was valued and that had long been our mantra. Even if you were the guy scoring all the tries, you gave credit to the blokes who got you the ball. It was so crucial to understand that in a game that relies so heavily on every person doing their job. Even when guys like Jonah Lomu were being lauded by the media during those early Hong Kong years, he, and they, were always uncomfortable at one player being singled out for attention. I loved that attitude. It's what makes a team strong.

There was another thing: my sevens teams always made time for people, no matter what the age. Whether it was at a kindergarten, primary school or rest home, our guys made a point of being impeccable ambassadors for the sport. Nothing was ever too much for them in terms of interacting with fans and supporters. I think it brought a lot of joy to the players to meet and greet the people who took an interest in them. It reminded them that they could inspire others.

As a team, we were inspired by the consistency of a core nucleus of players who acted as the spine of the programme. We had that group of sevens specialists – DJ Forbes, Tomasi Cama, Lote Raikabula and Tim Mikkelson, for whom sevens was their job. The work they did both in camp and on their own was exemplary and set the standard for everyone else. We were adding enthusiastic players to that mix, building depth with an eye to the next big tournament after Delhi – the Sevens World Cup.

Quite why the World Cup had been such a tough tournament for us to win was a mystery to me. I had thought long and hard about that over the years, but still could not quite pinpoint the underlying issue. In sevens, you can't win 'em all, but this tournament in particular was the toughest of nuts to crack. We had only been successful once since 1994, back in Argentina in 2001 when the boys had been inspired to play for their injured captain, Eric Rush. Short of breaking DJ Forbes' leg and hoping for the same response, I had no magic bullet. What I did have was that drive for increasing our playing stocks.

In 2012, understanding the need to build vital experience ahead of the World Cup the following year, we used 31 players across the tournaments. By contrast, in 2011, just 22 players were used in the season. It was a big percentage increase in personnel and an extraordinary number of guys to have coming in and out of camps, and in and out of selection favour. However, it was so important to the programme. Unlike during Commonwealth Games years, there was no chance to garnish the side with more high-profile Super Rugby players, so what we created within the environment would have to cover all bases for the Moscow showpiece in 2013.

The trick for all the players outside the main contracted servants of the game was to have them in the camp for long enough. Every team on the series was improving as their coaching methods developed and their player stocks increased, and the game itself was changing as a result. If we had thought fitness was paramount in the mid-1990s, the premium placed on it now was exponentially greater. The game had become more complex and more thoroughly analysed as well. Players weren't the problem – the preparation of players was the problem. The solution was to give them time in the environment.

After the success in Delhi, we had returned to the winner's circle in 2010/11 and 2011/12, taking the World Series crowns in both seasons. South Africa had begun to emerge as a genuine power in the sport at this time and we knew why – they had moved to centralise their sevens programme and that move was starting to pay dividends, as we would soon enough discover. Fiji, after a couple of uncharacteristically average years, were also on the comeback and in 2012 would push us all the way to the final tournament as we hung on to the series lead by the skin of our teeth. Ironically, our two Fijians – Tomasi and Lote – were often the difference. It never ceased to amaze me how much time they could buy in a game. It was the most Fijian trait of all, and something very few other players could ever master.

We were in good shape to hit the new season, and in May of 2012 I was also hit by a major surprise: I was inducted to the IRB Hall of Fame (now known as the World Rugby Hall of Fame). It was truly humbling for me to be honoured in this way by the governing body of the global game, and I was chuffed that the sport of sevens was being recognised at the same time. While I was the forty-ninth inductee, I was the first active coach to ever receive the honour, the panel deciding to override the rules which stipulated that all candidates would need a mandatory three-year stand-down period after their coaching or playing days were over to be considered for selection. I'm not sure what they were trying to say! Perhaps they thought I may not ever retire! Regardless, it was a touching moment to accept that prestigious honour on behalf of all the players who had been a part of my coaching career.

I got to catch up with many of them a few months later when the Bay of Plenty Rugby Union held a special tribute dinner for me in my home town of Tauranga. More than 40 former players attended the evening, with Eric Rush, Christian Cullen, Glen Osborne and others all taking turns at roasting their old coach in front of a great crowd. I was slandered at every turn that evening.

It was truly humbling
for me to be honoured
in this way by the
governing body of the
global game, and I
was chuffed that the
sport of sevens was
being recognised
at the same time.

The stories had grown as tall as Glen Osborne's hair had grown grey – he was still pissy with me for not including him in my all-time dream team! That same night, I was presented with the Key to the City of Tauranga which was another unexpected honour. The City Council had one more surprise up their sleeve as well: the field at Blake Park, where the Mount Maunganui Rugby Club hosts its home games and where my sevens teams had for years come to train in the shadow of the wind-blown pines that line the grass embankment, was to be renamed 'Gordon Tietjens Field'. I had spent almost half my life playing club rugby and coaching on that field and it was an incredible gesture of recognition.

The night itself is one I will never forget. To be surrounded by former players, family and friends – including my old sparring partner Tony Dykstra and my mentor Warwick Talbut – gave me an enormous sense of satisfaction, and there were one or two tears, I'll admit, when the players honoured me with a haka to close the evening. It was led by Eric, of course, with Peter Woods and Glen Osborne not far behind. Jonah, unfortunately, was not able to attend. Glen, rather unfairly, had passed on Jonah's apologies to the audience with the immortal line: 'He didn't know which one of his four wives to bring.'

There's one other thing that needs to be said about that night. I was late. I know what you're thinking: Who's late to their own testimonial dinner? Well, I'm afraid it simply couldn't be helped. There was a club sevens tournament that afternoon in Greerton, on the outskirts of Tauranga, and I had heard there were a couple of prospects who would be playing. I couldn't pass up the opportunity to see them for myself now, could I?

If we needed any further reminder that the World Series was more competitive than ever, the first five tournaments of the 2012/13 season was just that. Five different nations claimed victories over that period – ourselves included when we defeated France 47–12 in the South African event. Fiji, Samoa, England and South Africa also claimed titles as the series shot through Australia, Dubai, South Africa, New Zealand and the USA. We were consistent over this time, without being dominant, and made all but one of those finals. The elevation to tournament play of big forwards Scott Curry and Sam Dickson had been encouraging, while in South Africa, big Auckland winger Ben Lam was a one-man wrecking ball. We had also found a wonderful second playmaker in Hawke's Bay's Gillies Kaka, who was so laid back off the field that I was often tempted to check his pulse. On it, he was more alive than anyone, although at times he would do things that would affect my own pulse!

It was a side that had good pace, as well as confrontational ability, and, as our date with destiny in Russia approached, I was glad that we finished the series with a cup win in England and the overall title in the bag. It was no time for complacency, but the confidence boost was a timely one. We had unearthed some great players, had won a third straight World Series, and had a tight team dynamic that had maintained a high standard in training and in game output. I now had the unenviable task of selecting a team to take on the World Cup challenge. It was never an easy job, but at least I had the greatest resource any coach could ask for: plenty of choice.

15

—

WHAT GOES UP

IT WAS AN odd choice for a World Cup venue. No one would have said Moscow was a natural fit for the sport's marquee tournament, but the powers that be had made that decision and we would have to deal with it. It was a new experience for us all; none of us had been to Russia before, and we were also, for the first time, not alone. New Zealand had a couple of years earlier launched its Go For Gold campaign in a nationwide search to build a women's sevens team. The women's game had expanded rapidly in the last two years and they too would be playing their World Cup at Moscow's Luzhniki Stadium on the southwestern edge of the central city.

The stadium itself certainly had a backstory. Originally completed in 1956 as the Central Lenin Stadium, it was considered the national stadium of Russia, built with materials carted from every corner of that vast collection of republics. It had hosted many football matches over the years, including two Champions League finals, and was the main venue for the 1980 Olympic Games, capable of holding at that time a staggering 103,000 spectators. New Zealand had boycotted those Games in protest at the USSR's invasion of Afghanistan in 1979, though four athletes – canoeists Ian Ferguson, Alan Thompson and Geoff Walker, and modern pentathlete Brian Newth – attended and competed under the

New Zealand Olympic Committee flag.

The stadium's name had been changed to Luzhniki in 1992, derived from the term for the flood meadows surrounding its location. It was a fitting name, for it absolutely belted down on the day of the finals, the sparse crowd thankful that at least the seats were covered. You can't help the weather, of course, and everything else about the tournament – the training facilities, transportation and accommodation – was first class.

As for our play, first class wasn't exactly the way to describe the opening day. The 2013 Sevens Rugby World Cup was played over three days, and as I had already learned, three-day tournaments were great levellers due to the fact they reduced the number of games per day in pool play and gave greater recovery times to teams that perhaps wouldn't have the stamina required for a standard two-day event. We only had the one game on the first day – against Canada – and while the scoreline was comfortable in the end, there was an element of lethargy about the win that had me pacing the halls that night.

The team did not lack for ability. Although Scott Curry had been forced out through injury the week prior to leaving, I'd had an otherwise full roster to choose from when I had picked the squad. I wanted X-factor, and I had plenty of it at my disposal. Sam Dickson, Tim Mikkelson, Bryce Heem, Lote Raikabula and DJ Forbes provided plenty of punch, while Tomasi Cama and Gillies Kaka could spark any attack. As for the weapons for them to use, Pita Ahki, Kurt Baker, Waisake Naholo, David Raikuna and Sherwin Stowers represented a formidable arsenal. That said, we still had to make sure we used them properly.

The wake-up call duly came on day two. After a cruise-control win against Georgia, the USA was to be our final pool match and they came out absolutely fired up, shooting out to a 17–nil lead and threatening to leave our campaign dead in the water. We needed someone to create, and I made the decision to sub David Raikuna into the game. It was again a gut-feel decision, but I could sense that his footwork and acceleration just might be the key to unlocking the USA defence. It says plenty about the pressure we were under that at one stage, DJ pointed to the posts and Gillies took a penalty shot. Back then, I think I could have counted the number of penalty goals my sides had taken in previous games on the fingers of one hand! The decision caught me totally off guard, but it proved to be a good one. Combined with three converted tries, scored by Sherwin, Tim and David, we took the game 26–19 and with it advanced to the quarterfinals where we would face a Welsh team that had defeated Fiji earlier in the day.

I remember getting back to the hotel that night and sitting alone in the vast lobby café with my iPad, poring over footage as I searched for answers as to why we were blowing hot and cold. I put together in my own mind the contents of what would be my team talk to the boys before we headed out the next day for the quarterfinal. Ultimately, it all boiled down to the same thing it usually did with New Zealand teams – we were always good when we won the contact area and we had been far too passive in that department and overly reliant on the ball players to get us moving forward.

The following morning, we assembled in the team room to confront some home truths. I told them that I knew we had special players in the team but we had to stop shirking our work and start thinking as one. Ruthlessness was what we needed, not offloads. I had asked assistant coach Damian Karauna to put together clips of every player in the team doing the tough stuff. I knew they would respond to those visual cues and Damian did an exceptional job setting that to music for the boys. We finished that session with a team prayer as we always did on the way to finals. Almost all of the players were men of faith, and even those that were not, respected that moment and were only too willing to take part.

I asked Lote Raikabula to lead, but as we bowed our heads there was nothing but silence. I glanced up, just to make sure he was alright. When I did, I could see him, head bowed, tears streaming down his face. It was a signal to me that the boys would be okay that day. Lote was simply caught up in the emotion of the moment, and in the love he had for the team and the boys around him. He took a deep breath, led the prayer, and we left that room with a focus as fierce as I had ever known it. It was an amazing feeling, and Wales would have no answer when we finally took the field.

The victory would set up a semifinal with Fiji, which was always a sure-fire way to have the anxiety levels rising. It was a typically tight match, but it was destined for a very atypical disruption. Leading 7–nil at the break, after playing in some of the heaviest rain I can recall, the decision was made to postpone the start of the second half and get the players off the field. For the first time in history, an international sevens game was postponed due to a lightning strike. You really couldn't make this stuff up. It was so far-fetched that none of us knew what to do. We retreated to the changing rooms and had no choice but to sit it out, and listen to Kurt Baker cracking jokes. It was the longest hour I had experienced in coaching.

In fairness to Kurt, he was exceptional once the game was finally restarted. I was relieved. I had become extremely nervous during the forced break, fearing that Fiji would have had time to regain their composure and formulate a fightback. We had been playing well in the first half and there was a risk that our fire may have died in the downtime. As it turned out, it was still smouldering away, and we put two more tries on in the delayed second half to take the win 17–nil. The fact we had kept them scoreless was the most pleasing aspect. Defence wins tournaments. Ours had been exceptional.

We were on track, and into the final, where we were to face an England side that had express pace and a good coach in Ben Ryan. I had developed an intense rivalry with Ben over recent seasons, a rivalry that had sometimes spilled over into confrontation. At that stage, there was an underlying tension between us, largely because we were both such highly competitive coaches. Our arguments may have seemed silly in hindsight, but the nature of the World Series meant that teams were always in close proximity – at hotels and airports, on planes, and in game venues. There was always the risk that things could get heated . . .

———

One such incident was at Johannesburg Airport during a transit from Dubai to the South African leg of the World Series. The players were all connecting on two different flights, but as they needed to eat, meals had been organised for the teams in the departures area. But they were calling our flight. I enquired whether it would be possible for us to jump ahead in the food queue before we had to board, to which the organisers gave the okay. Ben Ryan was not impressed and, perhaps not understanding the situation, demanded we get to the back of the line. Jumping to the defence of my players, I leapt into the fray. We had a stand-up argument in the middle of the departure lounge!

Though the frost between us would eventually thaw, one thing would not change: I had enormous respect for his coaching ability and I knew I would have to work hard to develop the game plan to defeat his team. Having watched their semifinal against Kenya, I had seen that they kicked the ball deep. A lot. It was a good plan in the wet, especially when you had speedsters who could chase all day long and put pressure on the receivers. I had a feeling that nothing was going to change against us. The weather certainly hadn't improved, and in those conditions a good kicking game can go a long way towards winning.

In a stroke of good fortune, our changing room was equipped with a whiteboard. Remembering how well the boys had responded to the vision we had showed them earlier in the day, I picked up a marker and gathered the team around me. I told them it was going to be a footrace all day, and England were going to kick. At that, I took the marker and drew our structure on the board. Then I looked at Gillies and drew an X as far behind the first line as the dimensions would allow. That was to be where he was stationed all game long, 60 metres behind everyone else. We would be one short on the first defensive line, but our halfback would just have to cover.

Having Gillies there meant he could cover the kick and have time to bring the ball forward or return the favour. The rest of the team would not have to exhaust themselves chasing back, and they could be set for when Gillies countered. Gillies and Tomasi would have usually switched between halfback and pivot in the game, but Tomasi would have to assume both roles on his own. Gillies was

I remember getting back to the hotel that night and sitting alone in the vast lobby café with my iPad, poring over footage as I searched for answers.

at fullback, and that's where he would remain. Sure enough, when the game got under way, England kicked. And kicked. And kicked.

At halftime, we had a 17–nil lead. Gillies had been exceptional in the wet conditions, taking every kick that came his way and drilling them back. Our defence would then pin England in their own territory and force them to kick again. I was sure, during the break, that Ben would change tactics for the second half. Plan A certainly didn't seem to be working. Would they have the courage to keep trusting it, or would they find another way to come at us? I didn't know whether this was a great double bluff, or whether we really had them figured out.

As it turned out, England backed their Plan A, and we backed Gillies. When the full-time whistle blew the score was 33–nil, we had executed our game plan to perfection, and we were once again world champions. What made the win even sweeter was the fact the New Zealand women's side had also won their final, played directly before ours. I have to say, that certainly provided just a touch more motivation for the boys. They didn't want the girls to get all the glory that day. After the game, the two teams came together for a memorable photograph to capture the occasion. It truly was a great day for New Zealand sevens, and one of my favourite memories as a coach. It felt like a real coaching victory for me, given it had required a lot of faith in a very unorthodox game plan. The boys were over the moon and celebrated long into the night back at the hotel.

Waisake Naholo was especially overjoyed. In fact, he was so happy he returned home and named his new dog – an English bulldog – 'Moscow' in honour of the win. Speaking of all things English, Ben was eventually let go by England after a number of years at the helm which, in my opinion, was a massive mistake on their part. He would soon be picked up by another team, however, and in time he would get the last, long, laugh. Meanwhile, the Queen of England had a surprise for me. In her Birthday Honours List that month I was named a Knight Companion of the New Zealand Order of Merit. I was about to officially become Sir Gordon Tietjens.

I cannot tell you what a huge honour it was for me to be surrounded by close friends and family at Government House in Wellington for my investiture ceremony in September that year. I had never expected when I started out on this path 20 years before that something like this would ever be possible. I was blessed to have a job – two jobs – that I loved, and Warwick Talbut and his wife Lesley were also with me that day. I owed so much to him for giving me such freedom to pursue my passion, and I could tell he was as chuffed as I was during the ceremony. I felt it was an honour that belonged to so many people, especially to the players and everyone who had helped to grow the game of sevens over the last two decades.

It had been an extremely humbling year, between the Hall of Fame induction and now a knighthood. I was starting to wonder what I had done to deserve these accolades, really. I had merely fallen in love with a game and had somehow been blessed to coach it for much longer than I ever imagined I would. I was starting to worry that with all this fuss, someone might at any minute tell me I had done my time, and try to move me on.

I hoped not. Even then, all I was thinking about was the chance to go to the Olympic Games and to take a shot at winning a gold medal. I had thought about that since the sport successfully bid for inclusion in 2009. I had thought about it an awful lot. There was no way I was going to give up before I got that shot. For now, though, I was going to remain plain old 'Titch' and get back to the job. We had a Commonwealth Games tournament in Glasgow to think about. Although I was already formulating my plans, the Olympics would just have to wait.

After a three-peat of World Series titles, there was no reason to think we weren't on track for another as the new season quickly arrived in October 2013. That confidence was confirmed at the first tournament of the year, in Australia, where the boys went through the first five games conceding just one try, against England, in the semifinal. It was one of the best tournament performances I can recall; they had scored 145 points to five on their way to reaching the final. They scored 40 more in the last game, handing a heavy defeat to Australia on their home patch.

Success in sevens, as we had learned so often in the past, was a fickle mistress, and the following month in Dubai, despite having a settled squad that featured just three changes from Australia, we were mowed down by a rampant Fiji in the semifinal, conceding 44 points and failing to score any of our own. It was a timely reminder that the Fijians would never cease to be a threat in the sport, and that we could never sit back and rest on our laurels. Although we would go one better in South Africa, we would once again come up short, this time losing in the final to the host nation. In Las Vegas in January 2014, South Africa would again defeat us in the final.

There was something brewing between us and the 'Blitzboks' as they were known. They had a team that possessed so much natural pace that playing them required a superhuman defensive effort. One mistake and the likes of Cecil Afrika, Seabelo Senatla and Branco du Preez could score in an instant. Like us, they had a real power philosophy at the contact area as well, with hard-working forwards such as Kyle Brown and Kwagga Smith who could run all day and win plenty of turnovers. Because of the similarity between the two sides, it was always an intense contest, and one we were always thrilled to win, as we did in Wellington that February in front of a rapturous home crowd.

I had made the decision early that for that year's Commonwealth Games I would not be looking to bolster the squad with fifteens talent, as I had done previously. The fact was that we were in a good groove, with core players providing the stability and several years of developmental engineering affording us a wider pool of tournament experience. The last three tournaments of the season had all ended in success, and we claimed the Hong Kong title for the first time since 2011. It had always been such a tough tournament to win, and we had once again taught England a lesson in wet-weather sevens.

I was particularly happy with the form of a young Auckland kid by the name of Akira Ioane, who had debuted in Wellington earlier in the year. Akira and his younger brother Rieko were outstanding prospects and I had made a point of meeting with their parents Eddie and Sandra – both accomplished athletes in their own right – to get a sense of what made both boys tick. They were very different, both emotionally and physically. Akira was a powerful loose forward with incredible tackle-beating ability, while Rieko was a utility back with express speed and an incredible step. While Rieko's chance would come later, I had brought Akira into the team in 2014 and had worked diligently to make sure he was fit enough to make his talents count on the sevens field. From what I had seen in his first few tournaments, he had the potential to become one of the biggest names in the game.

As much as I was excited about some of the new faces, it was a couple of the familiar ones who would give me sleepless nights as I counted down to the selection of the Commonwealth Games team. Tomasi Cama and Lote Raikabula had been lynchpin players over a long period of time, having debuted in 2005 and 2006 respectively. Their vision for the game and sheer ability had so often been the difference in close matches, but I knew all those seasons in the team had taken a toll. They were still great players, but their light – once radiant and bright – had been ever so slightly dimmed. I agonised for many days about what had to be done, and ultimately named neither man in the team for Glasgow. I did, however, ask them both to join us for our final preparations in the seaside town of Castricum, to the northwest of Amsterdam, where we had been invited by local rugby aficionado Matts Marcker to fine-tune our game for the big tournament ahead. It was a beautiful part of the Netherlands, set back from the wide dunescape of the North Sea coast, with a picturesque rugby club ground that offered everything we needed in terms of training.

We even played a local selection in a last hit-out before leaving for Scotland, and more than 5000 fans descended on the park for the game. Before kick-off there was a moment of poignancy – a minute's silence for the 283 people who had lost their lives that week when a Malaysian Airlines flight from Amsterdam to Kuala Lumpur had been shot down over the Ukraine. The game was more exhibition than full contact, and it was good to soak up the festival atmosphere before having to face the reality of what lay ahead.

I had always loved visiting Scotland, and Glasgow was alive with Games fever when we arrived at the athletes' village. A boisterous town with a cheery disposition that had grown out of industrial roots, Glasgow was at its hospitable best in late July of that year. Even the much-maligned Scottish weather was playing its part, and the whole city seemed excited at the prospect of hosting such an important event. As for the sevens venue, Ibrox Stadium, home of Rangers Football Club, couldn't have been more perfectly designed for sevens. The sell-out crowd packed the grandstands and their proximity to the playing field created an electric atmosphere for the two days of play.

Although Lote and Tomasi had stayed behind in the Netherlands to provide last-minute injury cover, the arrival of Sherwin Stowers following the birth of his child back in New Zealand meant the pair would no longer be required for stand-by duty. It was tough on them and I felt their pain, but we had a team that was more than capable of winning a fifth straight gold medal. And the expectations on them to do just that were massive. None of the players wanted to be part of the first New Zealand side not to claim Commonwealth Games gold. I wondered whether they were too much fuelled by fear rather than motivated by opportunity, but DJ had told me that it was exactly how they had felt in Delhi four years earlier. I also wondered whether my own quest for perfection had only added to the pressure they felt.

We didn't have time to dwell on the emotional aspects, though, and soon enough were into pool play, first against Canada and then against the host nation. Although Canada were dispatched with clinical efficiency, Scotland proved a much tougher proposition. Test fullback Stuart Hogg was outstanding for them that day and

I wondered whether they were too much fuelled by fear rather than motivated by opportunity.

we had to dig deep to come out on top against a team that played hard and fast. It hadn't helped that we copped two yellow cards in the match, and at one stage played with just five men. Though I wasn't thrilled by the performance, or the discipline, I did think it could serve to shake any complacency from our game, just as the scare against the USA in the World Cup the previous year had done.

Barbados provided us with a reprieve in the final pool match, and we were able to rack up the points on them. More importantly, we had come through with no significant injuries and could approach the day of the finals with a renewed enthusiasm for the contest. The quarter- and semifinals were both tough games, against Kenya and Australia respectively. We had a big side, with the likes of Bryce Heem, Akira Ioane, Ben Lam and Scott Curry, and we needed them to be at their bludgeoning best to get us through those encounters. On the other side of the draw, South Africa were making things look a lot easier, putting 30 points on both Scotland and Samoa to earn a date with us in the gold-medal match. I knew it was going to be a game that required us to be at our very best. Yes, South Africa had strike power in the backline, but people unfamiliar with the intricacies of the game underestimated how good their forwards were at dominating the collisions and contact areas. I knew we had a great defensive heart that could cover their breakout capabilities. What I needed us to do was negate the influence of players like Kwagga Smith, who I thought was their real key to victory.

The boys were unbelievably focused as we prepared to run out onto the famous footballing pitch for the final. They knew exactly what they needed to do, and for vast periods of the game were in complete control of the tempo and direction of play. It was such an even contest, and South Africa were only able to snap the deadlock late in the game when they scored a wonderful breakout try. But I believed that if we could stay in the zone, and be patient, we could still win. The seconds seemed to stretch into an unknown dimension of time, passing simultaneously too fast and extraordinarily slow. How many tournaments had we won after the siren sounded? How many times had we done it on the last play of the game? I had lost count over the years, there had been so many irons pulled from fires.

Tick, tick, tick. Time was up on the clock, but we had the ball. Just be patient, I thought to myself, trying to stay calm on the sideline. One more play was all we needed, one more phase to finally crack the defence. Tim Mikkelson had the ball and threw a looping pass to Akira who was stationed perfectly in the middle of the park. It went through his hands and bounced away downfield. With it bounced our last chance to win. Our Commonwealth Games golden run had finished after 29 consecutive victories. We were still medallists, and that needed to be recognised, but I was crushed for the players, and especially for Akira who blamed himself for the loss. He should never have felt that way, especially given he was still just 18 years old. We were simply beaten by a better team on the day.

I was still very proud to see that team standing on the dais in the late evening light in Glasgow. Although it wouldn't be to the strains of New Zealand's anthem, they were still medallists. I knew they were disappointed, but that team had given until they simply had nothing left to give. That was good enough for me. I had kept a line from a report following the 2008 Wimbledon final between Rafael Nadal and Roger Federer. It was an epic five-set thriller – the best game of tennis I have ever seen. Afterwards Federer was devastated and in tears at the press conference. The line read: 'Nadal won the greatest game of tennis but Federer gained in defeat. He showed us that while losing is painful, it is not necessarily failure. How can it be when you've given it all you have?'

16
—

SO MANY QUESTIONS

WE NEEDED TO review what had happened in Glasgow. In sport, as in business, disappointment needs to be followed by swift and thorough analysis. Only by exploring every contributing factor can you expect to find pathways to improvement. We certainly looked at the way we had prepared and selected the team for the Commonwealth Games, though I was uncomfortable that the week spent in the Netherlands ahead of the Games came in for particular scrutiny.

I considered that it had given us an ideal base to work from. Yes, the surroundings were unfamiliar, but logistically everything had been well organised and the camp had run without hiccup. There had been a late call on Sherwin Stowers to join the team, but again, I saw no significant issue. He had experience, had won gold before with the team, and was supremely fit. The exclusion of Tomasi Cama and Lote Raikabula was also questioned, but in Tomasi's case, calf issues had plagued him in the lead-up to the campaign (and would ultimately lead to his retirement) and Lote just couldn't find the spark that he required. If anything, their non-selection was perhaps problematic in that the other, experienced guys knew two of their brothers wouldn't be with them. In the close-knit world of a sevens side, that can have a major impact.

I was no stranger to selection conundrums. Over the course of 20 years I'd had to make countless big calls on the players, all of them with due consideration and, with very few exceptions, the appropriate communication before and during the process. Of course, I hadn't got them all right and no coach ever does, but my hit rate had been pretty good and I had the results to back that up. Having sustained success over a long period of time serves to reinforce your instinct for selection, and I certainly felt that I had earned the right to say I was pretty good at understanding the needs of my teams for the demands of the schedule. My players knew that I had a job to do and that while I loved them all individually, I had to do what was right in the best interests of the team. There were some calls that they wouldn't like, or might not fully understand, but I underpinned my coaching approach with what I thought was a keen eye for discontent and a knack for making sure I was as consistent as I could be in terms of the standards I demanded from all of them. There are few guarantees in sport, and the best athletes are the ones that never lose perspective on where they stand in relation to the benchmark.

The Commonwealth Games had confirmed one thing to me: the Olympics would require us to build an even more competitive training environment in which no place was guaranteed. That may have seemed unfair on the men who had committed full-time to sevens, but if they continued to set the standards they were capable of, their selection would take care of itself.

As yet another World Series began, I wrote my player wish list. There was no doubt in my mind that players would jump at the chance to become Olympic athletes, regardless of the myriad stories about how hard sevens training was, or where the sport sat in the pecking order of New Zealand rugby. As I was soon to find out, not everyone shared my enthusiasm and respect for the Olympic Games.

———

There were a number of factors at play during this period that all served to make it feel like a frantic time of my life. For starters, I had to get my team back into World Series mode quickly after the silver medal in Glasgow. I knew they had been down after that, and that we would have to deal with the inevitable turnover of personnel before we could get back to the basics of hard work on the training field. At the same time, I had to start thinking ahead to the 2016 Olympics and the logistical minefield that was still to be navigated around player availability and training programmes. I wanted as little disruption as possible to the day-to-day workings of the team, but was cognisant of the fact players were always talking to each other, their agents and others in the game, and there was no doubt rumours would start swirling about which players I was targeting and what that might mean for the team.

There was something else: I found that there had been a shift in the outlook of the players. I didn't know whether I had failed to cross some kind of new generational divide, or whether the players were simply tired from the demands of the programme, or whether there was a growing sense of uncertainty around the Olympic Games, but it was a very real feeling. All of a sudden, things were not what they used to be. I suspected, fairly or unfairly, that a new focus on player empowerment, which had been promoted to us by the New Zealand Rugby High Performance team on the back of the All Blacks' philosophies, may have contributed to this new, strange atmosphere. Modern developments, such as leadership groups, increased player consultation and coaches' meetings, had me feeling less in control.

In years past I had always communicated plans around training with the captain of the side, and had full faith in him to get the team on board and drive the effort. I believed that by giving my leader an insight into the philosophies behind the design of each block of training, they would be in a position to support me and to back my judgement when the heat really started to come on. We never had meetings for the hell of it, or to tick organisational boxes, we simply got down to work. Now, more and more, I found that the captain and the players in the new leadership group wanted an input into the content of the training, the intensity of the training – exactly how hard we were training – and the duration of each training session.

I was unapologetic about being hypodermic in my approach to fitness and in my feelings about the intensity that I thought we needed to be training at. It had worked for me for so long, and I saw no reason that it wouldn't continue to work if we could get the buy-in from the team. I had good reasons to demand extra work in areas where there were clear deficiencies. If trainings weren't accurate, we needed to address it. If players were slipping in their fitness levels, we needed to put in more effort. There was no short cut to success, no way a softer option was going to be a better option in a sport that demands peak conditioning.

More and more people, it seemed, were involved in every decision. That had the potential to destabilise, rather than strengthen, our environment. I understood that there were elements of the All Blacks culture that were useful for us in the sevens programme, but I had bottom lines that were non-negotiable and always had been. I was always keen to learn from the best, to take parts of successful strategies and use them for the benefit of the team. But they had to be moulded to fit the sevens arena. We were different in the size and scale of our organisation, and there was a range of different demands on our players, both mentally and physically. We had a very different logistical challenge to our season, and we faced the daily reality of hiding in plain sight of the New Zealand rugby public. There was no way we could ever subscribe to a common methodology. We were a very uncommon rugby team.

As a coach, you have to be able to understand your players' motivations and the pressures – both internal and societal – that they feel exposed to. I thought I had a handle on that, but I was starting to see that there was a shift in the balance in the side. I found that there were more questions than ever before about what we were trying to achieve. I was not convinced that they were the right questions, or whether they were being asked for the right reasons. I was asking some questions of my own around how much of a priority sevens really was within New Zealand Rugby. We had started the 2014/15 season with early exits in Australia and Dubai, and a final defeat in South Africa, but hit the new year with victory in Wellington where Rieko Ioane made his debut in fine style, scoring two tries in a thrilling final against England. Unfortunately, it was not the tournament it used to be. The crowds had waned substantially and it felt in every way like we were late to our own party. While we were happy for the win, it was a shame for the players in many ways. In its heyday, Wellington rivalled any tournament in the world for atmosphere. By 2015, the balloon had well and truly popped.

It was Rugby World Cup year and the All Blacks were ramping up their campaign to become the first team to win back-to-back titles. We knew sevens would be even further back down the publicity bus in a year like that, but we still needed to firm up our plans for potential players to join the training programmes. I had, at New Zealand Rugby's behest, filed with them my player requests, and was eager to get a take on the interest levels around the game. Neil Sorensen, the general manager of rugby, had agreed to ask each of the players if they would be keen to have a crack. I was thrilled to hear that around three-quarters of those players had expressed an interest, backing up my assumptions that the Olympics would be a great drawcard.

I had not been shy in asking. Guys like Beauden Barrett, Ben Smith and Malakai Fekitoa were certainly targets, as was Ardie Savea and even Kieran Read. I well remember ringing Kieran and I think he almost fell over when I asked if he would be keen. He had never been a part of the sevens environment, but I figured with his speed and size there was no harm in asking. He took a couple of days to consult with others, but the chance to captain the All Blacks in 2016 was hard for him to turn down, as I could rightly understand. He still got a buzz out of being asked, which pleased me greatly.

The one stipulation I had, which was agreed to by New Zealand Rugby, was that any player who was interested in making the Olympics team had to commit to four tournaments in 2016 – the first two in New Zealand and Australia, which clashed with the Super Rugby pre-season, and the last two in Paris and England, which impacted on the Super Rugby round robin. It served a dual purpose. First, it was only fair to the full-time sevens players who were busting arse all year on the series that any player under consideration prove their worth in tournament play. Second, the days of waltzing into a sevens team on reputation were long gone. Teams were better organised, far more competitive, and fitter than they had ever been before. Players needed game time to come to terms with the modern shape of sevens attack and defence. And there was, as always, the fitness element to consider.

After the initial positive response, there had been a long period of radio silence. I was keen to know where I stood so I could continue to work on plans for camps and training modules. There was something else, too. I was concerned about where the training was in terms of fitness work. I had clashed a couple of times with our trainer Mark Harvey on stylistic issues and was keen to sort that out and move on in the same direction. I was keen to let Mark do what he did best – it was his area of expertise – but there were times when I thought the guys simply weren't sevens fit or getting the miles I wanted. Mark had been concerned about the training load and its impact on soft-tissue injuries, but I came back time and time again to what I knew worked. It was sixteen 150s and time on feet.

I had to trust Mark because that side of team preparation was all him. That said, I had been around long enough to know what I needed from the players. After reading a medical paper that found the style of training I favoured actually reduced the kinds of injuries Mark had been concerned about, we came to an agreement that we would move back to the tried and tested. It was important that we were on the same page. I needed my management team to be a single voice in what would be a complex period for the team.

———

The Wellington victory would be our only one of the season. Although we would make cup finals in the USA, Hong Kong and Scotland, we would be defeated on each occasion by a resurgent Fijian team, still smarting from their Commonwealth Games exclusion. The sanction on Fijian athletes at the Games, which had been in place since the 2010 event, had been lifted in May of 2014, but it was by then too late for the Fijian side to enter the tournament. They played some exceptional sevens that season and were deserved World Series champions. There was no doubt that the Olympics was very much in their thinking. What a way that would be to make up for the Commonwealth Games snub.

We finished third in the series, behind Fiji and South Africa. It was the first time since the 2010/11 series that we had not claimed the overall crown, and it showed there was an enormous amount of work ahead of us before the crucial 2015/16 season started. In the meantime, I was still trying to get answers on what players were available to me, and a number of players who had initially expressed interest were, weeks later, showing a complete change of heart. One of those players was Beauden Barrett. I had spoken to Beauden personally at the behest of his manager and in our conversation I felt he was very keen to be a part of our programme. Remember, this was a kid who had first played for me fresh out of school and had always impressed with his enthusiasm and work ethic. I had finished that phone call feeling very positive about where he was at. Several days later, he was a no-go.

One by one, I got word that players were changing their minds. I felt for those players. In my view, it seemed they were being encouraged to maintain their Super Rugby work or to be a part of the All Blacks' plans for the 2016 June series against Wales. I didn't know for sure who was making the calls, but after the All

Blacks played Argentina in Christchurch in July of 2015, I thought I had a chance to find out. I had a meeting scheduled with the All Blacks coaches, Steve Hansen and Ian Foster, Don Tricker, Neil Sorensen and New Zealand Rugby CEO Steve Tew the morning after the test match to once and for all sort out what players would be available. It was ostensibly a negotiation, though it felt more like a Dickensian production. I was Oliver Twist, and there was no way I was getting more. Steve Hansen seemed to not be in the best frame of mind after Waisake Naholo had been injured in the test, and faced with his own fresh dilemma, I got the distinct feeling my needs were not his major concern. That said, I too needed some clarity. It had to be dealt with now.

I soon realised I had absolutely no power in that meeting. Steve Hansen wanted to know why I required Ben Smith for four tournaments. In his mind, Ben was good enough as it was. I explained to him that to be good at the game, you have to be playing it, and Ben hadn't played sevens since 2010. I wouldn't budge on that, and therefore I had no Ben Smith. When we talked about Beauden Barrett, I asked if anyone could tell me why a guy who seemed so keen initially had now completely changed his mind. Neil Sorensen looked at Ian Foster and asked him what he had talked to Beauden about. Ian said he had never told him he couldn't play sevens, he had only outlined a list of things he needed to work on in the fifteens game. Given the All Blacks were about to lose a lot of experience in the midfield, when we discussed Malakai Fekitoa I wasn't surprised that Steve Hansen left me in no doubt that I wasn't having him.

I eventually left the meeting feeling completely isolated and that no leadership had been shown there. New Zealand Rugby had a documented strategic goal that proclaimed gold medals in the men's and women's sevens competition to be the number-one priority in the 2016 season. I was therefore very surprised that no one spoke up to defend the programme, or my right to prepare players as I saw fit. A couple of months after the meeting, once I was back to my own preparations, I received a text message from Neil Sorensen. He wrote: 'I admire you for the way you handled the disgrace that was the AB-7's selection issue. Your integrity remains intact.'

After that meeting, there was no doubt in my mind that sevens had absolutely no priority at all in New Zealand Rugby, not even for an event as important as this. It was both a depressing and infuriating realisation, and it wouldn't be the last time a player had a change of heart, as I would discover after the Australian tournament in January.

For now, though, I simply had to get on with preparations for the new season. I had secured the services of Augustine Pulu, Liam Messam and Sonny Bill Williams, which was a great positive, and the Ioane brothers were also all in. Kurt Baker had expressed his desire to return to sevens after trying his hand one last time at a Super Rugby gig with the Highlanders, and I still had that core playing group around which everything else could be built. It would need a new captain, however. DJ Forbes had decided to stand down.

DJ had been a warhorse for the New Zealand Sevens team since making his debut in the 2006/07 season. He was one of the greatest players ever to don the black jersey and he was also one of the most loyal and hard-working men I had ever had the pleasure to coach. He was also a realist. We both knew that he was struggling to maintain his high standards after so many years of play, and something had to give. I, more than anyone, wanted him to get to the Olympics, and we both agreed that maybe some time to focus on his own game would be better.

Just as it had been with Eric Rush when he called time, I told DJ that there was no way I was going to make that decision for him. We had been through too much and achieved too much together. It had to be his call. He had earned that right. In August 2015, he made the announcement that he was handing over the captaincy. It must have been such a tough call for him to make, and his courage to make it showed how much character he possessed. He didn't want to be at the Olympics because he was captain. He wanted to be there on merit. And he was tenacious enough to ensure that he was.

We discussed at length within the management group who we thought would be able to fill DJ's shoes. We came to the conclusion that Scott Curry should be his replacement and Scott accepted the honour which at least gave us some certainty heading into the season. What we could never foretell was that Scott would be badly injured in just the second tournament and would spend every remaining second of the 2015/16 season trying desperately to be fit enough for selection. As for the team, along with losing Scott, we would also suffer back-to-back losses to the USA in the first two tournaments. There was no better illustration of what the upcoming Olympic debut was doing for the sport of sevens in countries like the USA. It was also a timely reminder to us that we were only ever a couple of injuries away from having our season turned upside down. I couldn't wait to put those results behind us and get back to Wellington for the New Zealand leg. Fortunately, the losses were largely overlooked by New Zealand rugby fans. The

All Blacks had just become world champions again, and it always pays to accentuate the positive.

The new year brought new hope. While Scott had been a major loss, I finally had my hands on all the players from outside the programme who had wanted to take a shot at the Games, and they trained exceptionally well in the lead-up to Wellington. We would get the win at home again, with a last-minute try against South Africa in the final. A week later, we repeated the dose in Sydney. I was always rapt when we were able to win games like that because it showed that we were in good condition and could play right to the final whistle and beyond if necessary. Ardie Savea, Rieko Ioane, Ben Lam and Augie Pulu were outstanding over those two events, but Augie had suffered a broken arm in Sydney, adding to our growing injury list. It would get worse. During the North American leg in Canada that March, I learned that Ben Lam had been badly injured in a development game for the Blues. He was out of contention. Joe Webber had also been forced out and had undergone shoulder surgery.

I needed to find solutions to the growing casualty ward, and on 11 March, I sent an email to Don Tricker and Neil Sorensen. In it, I outlined my concerns about losing players like Joe and Ben and what that meant for the fortunes of the team. 'I can honestly tell you,' I wrote, 'I am desperately in need of some support to secure some quality players who can compete at the highest level to win a gold medal in Rio. With due respect to my current players, especially in the backs, we will not be good enough. I need players with some game-breaking qualities built around a more direct game as was displayed in Wellington and Sydney.' I listed players I would like to consider, once again including Beauden Barrett and Ben Smith and adding Vaea Fifita, Julian Savea, Seta Tamanivalu, Sione Fifita, Jone

Macilai, Patrick Osborne, Vince Aso and Nehe Milner-Skudder. I even enquired as to whether I might be able to consider Charles Piutau and Frank Halai, who had left New Zealand rugby but who I had contacted already to gauge their enthusiasm. I also pointed out that Ardie and the Ioane brothers still had to get through tough Super Rugby games before they returned.

It was a plea for help, really, from a desperate coach. I did not receive a single reply. Instead, not long after that email was sent, I received a phone call from Ardie Savea. He was out, too. I cannot tell you how devastated I was to receive that news. Here was a guy who only weeks before had told me how much he was enjoying the environment and how excited he was to get himself into the best physical shape for the Olympics. Now he was telling me he was refocusing on the fifteens game. I didn't need to ask him for an explanation, so I wished him luck and left it at that. It was yet another dagger in the chest. And fate had not finished with me. In Hong Kong, I lost DJ Forbes and Sam Dickson. I had no idea how I was going to pick a team for Rio.

17

ALL SHE WROTE

I HAD ALWAYS prided myself on keeping things simple. It had served our side incredibly well over the last two decades and we had created a formula for success that was based around a good leader, a giant dose of humility, hard work, character and respect. We had been an uncomplicated side, happy to get on with the job knowing that we had a great nucleus of players who would always teach the new boys the ropes. Players came and went, and all that was expected of them was that they pushed themselves to the limit and showed pride in the jersey.

What was once simple had now become an unwieldy mess. I had players out with injury, including my squad captain, other players who would only be rejoining the side for the final two tournaments before the Olympics, fringe players who had been drafted in to plug holes in the side, and it was by now abundantly clear that despite all the talk from New Zealand Rugby about priority for sevens and the premium placed on winning gold medals, no major-name reinforcements would be coming to the rescue for us. What had started as a dream had morphed into a full-blown nightmare, and out of this horror show I somehow had to back every instinct I had to select a team that was capable of winning.

I had always tried to remove emotion when I picked players,

but I felt I was running on emotion and not much else. On 3 July 2016, after finishing third once again in the World Series, I named my team for Rio. Despite the fact that nearly all of them had faced a battle to recover from injury, I picked my regular core of players. Scott Curry, Sam Dickson, DJ Forbes, Tim Mikkelson, Gillies Kaka and Joe Webber all would get their chance to become Olympians. Akira and Rieko Ioane, Sonny Bill Williams and Augie Pulu would also be rewarded for their decision to commit. It was also a big day for youngsters Teddy Stanaway and Regan Ware who rounded out the side, with Sione Molia and Lewis Ormond travelling as reserves.

There was one player who I agonised over more than any other, and that was Kurt Baker. He had always performed for me over a long period of time. Sure, he had some games that weren't as good as others, but generally speaking you always knew what you were going to get from him. He had a massive tank, for starters, and that is half the battle with so many players who have the requisite skills. Kurt was one of the great characters and had won me big tournaments with big plays since his debut in 2008. Kurt had been playing well but he had been under a massive injury cloud with hip flexor and Achilles issues and simply couldn't get the training under the belt. Despite my fondness for the man, I was concerned that if he could only get through one day of training, how could he cope with three days of games. I still wanted to take him as a travelling reserve, but as was his prerogative, he turned down the offer. As things would turn out, if he had joined us, he would have got the chance to play. He was extremely disappointed after being left out, and I understood that. I had a lot of respect for Kurt and I'm sure he had a lot for me, but he was genuinely hurt and that was understandable. I wish he had come. He deserved his shot.

The naming of the team was cathartic in a way, as at least it was now one thing that was set in stone. We could put the uncertainty of the last 18 months behind us and, barring disaster, get on with the job of preparing for the tournament as one. The plan was to fly to Florida and spend a week acclimatising to the heat while staying and training at the state-of-the art IMG Academy in Bradenton. It was a spectacular venue and should have given us the perfect preparation time for Rio. We had organised to play a couple of warm-up games against the USA and in the first game we came out and played exceptionally well. I thought I could see the spark returning to the team, and then we lost Teddy Stanaway to injury.

I didn't enjoy wallowing in self-pity but I didn't know how many more cruel twists I could take. That evening, I spoke with Don Tricker about replacements. I knew that Ardie Savea, Beauden Barrett and Ben Smith had all signed accreditation forms for the Games and had given an undertaking that they could be available if we had late injuries. Ardie and Beauden had a Super Rugby final to consider, but Ben Smith's Highlanders had been knocked out of the playoffs. He was the guy I wanted. Don told me he would call Ben, and that he would also touch base with Steve Hansen.

It finally came back that Ben thought he wouldn't be fit enough and that flying from Australia to South Africa and then back to South America would not be the right preparation for such a crucial event. In any case, his wife was due to give birth and he did not want to miss that moment. I accepted all of that, but was left to wonder what might have been if he had been available from the start. With that option closed, I called Liam Messam over as injury cover and Lewis Ormond was promoted to the full team.

The following day we came out, got soundly beaten in a second warm-up game through a lack of effort, and I was at my wits' end.

It was following that warm-up loss that we met with Don Tricker as a management team and I voiced my frustration at where the team seemed to be at. It was here where I finally had enough of the constant comparison to the All Blacks, where I finally broke down after 18 months of fret and worry. It was here that I resolved to address the team. I knew that so many of them had also endured months of uncertainty but it was time we all put it behind us. That day, I laid it all out.

Speaking plainly, I said we wouldn't even look like getting any kind of medal if we were going to prepare like we prepared that day. I needed these guys to switch on and wake up to the fact that we were going to be in the fight of our lives in a few days' time. I just needed them to get with the programme, to sharpen up in all areas of attitude. We had been considered for any number of years the best sevens team in the world, and we needed to start living that reputation. The mindset needed to be different. Everything we did from that point on had to be about optimising our chances of winning a gold medal. Every training run was about enhancing our combinations, every meal was about properly fuelling our bodies, every gym session was about coming out the other side a better athlete. Even our appearance needed work – which may have sounded old-fashioned, but I wanted the team to look like a team. I wasn't there to tell them what to wear – I had spent enough time telling them how far to run and what to eat – but to me their slipshod approach to attire was symbolic of a wider problem around pride and self-image.

Later that afternoon, I wandered over to the gym to watch them go through a session with Mark Harvey and I couldn't believe what I saw. They had obviously decided they would heed my counsel and had dressed for the gym in the exact same uniform: full hoodies and tracksuit pants. It must have been 30 degrees outside and even in the air-conditioned gym they were drenched in sweat. I couldn't believe what I was seeing. It showed me that we lacked genuine leadership. If this was what empowering players was all about, I was glad to be unsubscribed.

A few days later we were on our way to Rio, and to the Olympic Games. What a fraught journey it had been to get here, but despite everything, the moment we set foot in the athletes' village there was a sense of arrival. Sevens really was on the big stage. A sport that had begun life as a Scottish rugby club fundraiser was now a part of the biggest show of all. I could sense that the players were happy to have made it, and I relaxed a little knowing that I had trusted these guys so often before and I could trust them again. I was hoping that being in that amazing environment with its apartment towers and thousands of athletes from all over the world would provide the boost the team needed heading into the first day of action at the Deodoro Stadium. The venue was an hour's drive from the athletes' village, and looked an absolute picture. It was small and intimate by comparison with some of the stadia we were accustomed to, but the weather was perfect and I thought we looked ready to go. Japan, our first opponents of the Games, had other ideas.

If I had done my best to hide any residual fears I had after the Miami incident, they were all being realised in front of me on that playing field. Japan simply flew out of the blocks, scoring early to take a 7–nil lead. Shell-shocked, we took some time to find our feet, and eventually hit the front with two tries of our own. They came at a cost, though. After everything else we had been through, Sonny

Bill Williams had torn his Achilles and was out of the tournament. Not long after, Joe Webber also succumbed to injury and was also ruled out. We were possums in the headlights after that. Japan roared back and scored another try, which was also converted. At 12–14, we were staring down the barrel of one of the greatest upsets in the game's history. Sure enough, Japan clung on for the win.

It was a massively deflating experience for the guys but our policy in the team had always been to pick ourselves up and get on with the job. We still had two pool matches to play – against Kenya and Great Britain, and every chance of making the quarterfinals. Yet, if we had been taught a lesson in poor starts against Japan, it hadn't sunk in by the time we took on the Kenyans. Again, it was the opposition who made the early running, and it took a yellow card to Kenya's Collins Injera to get us motivated to score. Score we did and eventually we were able to stretch out to a 28–5 victory. We could take stock of the day, with our final pool game scheduled for the following morning. Taking stock might better be described as counting the toll. Scott Curry's nightmare of a season had got worse. He, too, was now out of the Games.

It is hard to describe the feeling in the camp that night. Our captain and two of our strike weapons were lost to us, we were facing a potential do-or-die final pool game the next day, and very little had gone right for us on the field. Despite the win against Kenya, it was all fits and starts in the first day. The team just needed to decompress and recover. Tomorrow would be a tough day, with only three reserves left in the side. We were going to have to go to the well, as we had done countless times before.

As it turned out, the well was all but dry. In the final pool match, Great Britain again took advantage of our poor starts, shooting out to a 21–nil lead early in the first half. The boys showed great character to fight back with three tries of their own, but one missed conversion would prove the difference and we crashed to our second defeat of pool play. Survival now became purely mathematical. Fiji would face the USA in their final pool game and would need to win by five points or more to help us into the quarterfinals – ironically, where we would face them should they win the match.

It is a terrible feeling to have your destiny in the hands of your arch-rivals, but the irony of the situation was just the icing on the cake. I have been nervous on many occasions watching my team play, but I can't recall ever being as nervous watching another team. One Fijian try could be the difference between making the quarterfinals and having the first pool-stage exit of my 22-year career. Surely, I thought, after all the doom and gloom, we must be due a ray of sunshine. Fiji eventually won the game, holding on to that magic five-point lead as the USA threw everything at them. In the wash-up of the pool stage, we were into the quarterfinals. How close were we? A one-point differential advantage over the USA.

Sevens had become such a ruthless game that making it to the playoff stages meant all bets were off. Any team was capable of an upset from here, and we had experienced these kinds of turnarounds so often in the past. Yes, we were playing Fiji, a team that had over the last couple of seasons been our tormentor-in-chief, but we knew how to beat them, and despite being short on manpower we could do it again. I was up against my old mate Ben Ryan, who had overseen the resurgence of the Fijian side. They perhaps had an even greater motivation than us at those Games. No Fijian athlete or team had ever won an Olympic medal.

With a depleted squad and nothing to lose, we ran out in the Rio rain for the quarterfinal. Again, we would be stung early by

I have been nervous
on many occasions
watching my team
play, but I can't recall
ever being as nervous
watching another team.

an opening try, and soon after, Rieko Ioane was sin-binned for a tip tackle. Remarkably, and showing every ounce of spirit that had made the team so successful for so long, we held the Fijians out with six men and then scored just before the break thanks to some Gillies Kaka magic. We were in this game – leading 7–5 in fact – and at halftime I implored the boys to get a hold of that slippery ball and take the game by the scruff of the neck. Ben Ryan may well have given his side the same message, for they were the ones who controlled possession in the second half, scoring a second try to reclaim the lead and make the score 12–7. With time up and one last chance to level the game, we were penalised while hot on attack. Fiji booted the ball to touch, and our first Olympic medal quest was over.

I was proud of the fight we had shown in that quarterfinal, and prouder still that the team put in everything they had in the fifth-place playoff against Argentina. It was Gillies' last game for the side and I was glad they sent him off on a high note. As for the campaign, well, it was a nightmare realised from start to finish. As one report stated after the event: 'Rugby was given a rebirth in Rio, and New Zealand didn't make the delivery room.' It was shattering for everyone in the team, especially as we had never lost hope in spite of every misfortune we had suffered. Later that evening, Fiji would defeat Great Britain 43–5 to win the gold medal. As much as I was devastated for us, I was also thrilled for Fiji. Having visited that beautiful nation so many times, I knew that moment was a life-changer for those men. They were the heroes of their country, immortals. Some weeks later, Ben Ryan would be given a chief's title and his own plot of land in a tropical paradise. Last laughs don't get much louder than that.

Meanwhile, as we dealt with the heartache of our failure in Rio, Steve Hansen fronted a press conference back in New Zealand. When asked about our campaign and the player availability issue, he told the gathered media: 'There's a definite conflict and it's been difficult for the players. Some of them have chosen to go, and some to stay, and that's been a decision they've had to make themselves without the influence of either Titch or myself.'

I spent the next few days reflecting on everything that had happened over the past 18 months. Had I done enough as a coach to get these guys in the best shape possible? Should I have been more assertive with New Zealand Rugby in terms of what I needed? Had I lost the faith and trust of the players? Or did everything – the injuries, disruption, uncertainty, anxiety – about this campaign serve to crush our most valuable asset: our unity? There had been a lot of talk about a review process after the Olympics, but if there was one, I wasn't a part of it. I came back to a vacuum, really. I was contracted until the end of the year, but realised I wouldn't be renewing my New Zealand contract after that. I offered to help in some capacity but there was little appetite for it. Later it would transpire that Scott Waldrom, who had once played for me in the side, would take the reins as caretaker coach until New Zealand Rugby's preferred new coach, Clark Laidlaw, worked out his contract in English rugby. I believed that said everything about how sevens was treated; if it was of genuine importance to New Zealand Rugby, then surely they would have their choice of coach in place for the new season.

As it was, the only real dissection of my final campaign had come in the form of an email from Tony Philp, a member of Don Tricker's High Performance team at New Zealand Rugby. It was four questions long and focused mainly on how our game plan had worked, and what hadn't, in Rio. There was no discussion of anything to do with the lead-up, or the player availability issue. I replied to his questions as best I could, and signed it off with an invitation to call me to discuss anything further. The phone did not ring. There was no hint of an independent review process, or any acknowledgement of the wider issues around leadership and management. I felt it was an opportunity missed. In any business, you thoroughly review your disappointments. It's how you constantly improve. If there was no appetite for a review, how could there be an appetite for future success?

In early September, I decided to officially resign as New Zealand Sevens coach. I was happy for the local paper to simply run the story and that could be that, but I called New Zealand Rugby to inform them of my decision and was asked by Don and his team to come to Wellington to hold a press conference with Steve Tew followed by a review of the campaign. I flew to the capital and on 6 September I announced that I was stepping down. Afterwards, Neil Sorensen, Don Tricker, Tony Philp and I sat in the Arabica café and made small talk. There was no review. I flew home to Tauranga that day, and went back to the office. There was work to be done and clients to catch up with. I was Gordon Tietjens, sales rep. And I was happy to be home.

18
—

GOING AROUND AGAIN

I LOVED SEVENS from the moment I was introduced to it. It was a game that embodied everything I loved about competitive sport. It required discipline and stamina, speed and skill – all in equal measure – and once I had tasted it, I knew it would be the dish I would dedicate my life to perfecting. The recipe for perfection, as I came to learn, is a tough one to follow. Sevens is a game that challenges preconceptions, one that hides its myriad complicated nuances in a cloak of simplicity. On the face of it, sevens is a sentence without the punctuation marks, a version of rugby liberated from the set-piece pauses of the fifteen-a-side format. Dig a little deeper, though, and it is a sport that writes its story in a very specific code, one which takes time to master and to decipher. Just when you think you have it figured out, it conspires to confound you all over again.

I thought about all that on a short flight from Auckland to Apia, the capital city of the island nation of Samoa where, in the spring of 2016, I would sit down with the Samoan Rugby Union to discuss plans to reignite their sevens programme. I thought about all I had learned, all I had committed to memory, all the plays we had developed, and all the players who had spent time in my teams as I had honed my craft over two decades in charge of the most successful sevens nation the game had ever known. I thought, too, about how all of that acquired knowledge could be used again.

———

After more than two decades in charge of New Zealand, I wondered if I would ever have the passion to coach another national side. I was a Kiwi, through and through, still counted pulling on the black jersey for the New Zealand Sevens team back in 1983 as the singular sporting achievement of my playing career, and for more than a third of my life I had dedicated what coaching acumen I had to helping my country achieve on the world stage. Even if another offer came through, would I really be prepared to coach against my own country?

The offer did come, very shortly after my return to New Zealand from Rio, and from an unexpected quarter. It was Rugby Canada, as their union is known, who contacted me initially, first paying me a visit in my home town of Tauranga and then flying me to Victoria in British Columbia to discuss with me the chances of guiding their programme through the next Olympic cycle. Canada had become a mainstay on the World Series circuit, and was a team that had grown a reputation as a genuine threat to any nation. On their day, the Canadian side could be blisteringly good on attack and staunch on defence, but ultimately they had missed out on qualifying for the Olympic Games and, obviously stung by that fact, their governing body saw an opportunity to build on what was a credible team desperate to be more than sporadically successful.

It was not an unappealing proposition. My teams had faced Canada innumerable times over the course of World Series play, and I had respect for their programme and an inkling that I could indeed help them take a step up in class. The only challenge would be distance, and I knew that after so many seasons away from family and so many months a year away from my wife, the pilgrimage to Canada would be a big ask. I promised to give the proposal due consideration, and with that decided, I returned to New Zealand where I took another phone call – this time from much closer to home.

The Samoan Sevens team had once been a force to be reckoned with. In the early days of my coaching tenure with New Zealand, they had already forged a reputation as a powerful and popular presence at the Hong Kong Sevens, winning the title the year before I was appointed to the head coaching role. Throughout the first 10 years of the World Series they were a team best avoided in knockout play, and had gone on to win the series in 2009/10 after dominating four of the eight tournaments that season. Since then, the programme had gone backwards as more and more players were drawn away from the game, having been contracted to clubs in the professional fifteens leagues in England, France, Japan and, of course, New Zealand.

There was also the not insignificant matter of funding – the Samoan Rugby Union had long struggled to compete financially and this fact only exacerbated the exodus of playing stocks from Samoa and from sevens. The union wanted to reverse their fading fortunes on the playing field, and felt that in the sport of sevens they had their best chance to reinvigorate both the players and the public. When they called, I was all ears.

Practically speaking, the three-hour flight from Auckland to Apia was a damn sight more attractive than the idea of long-hauling my way to Canada, but there was another, much more important, reason for considering making an application for the job with Samoa. In my time as coach of New Zealand, I had selected and trained many Pacific Island players. They had done so much for the sport – and for rugby in general – in New Zealand, and they had added enormously to me as a person. New Zealand rugby, and certainly the country's sevens programme, owed an inestimable amount to the contribution of Pacific players. I knew how devastated the team and its fans had been when they, too, had missed qualification for the Olympic Games, and I also knew that what had made Samoa's World Series win in 2009/10 so special was that every player in the team had been based in Samoa. With the right coaching and the right systems in place, I believed from the very first conversation that they could recreate that level of success. All they needed was someone who was prepared to look within as much as without to unearth that bountiful talent.

It was a challenge that the more I thought about it, the more it excited me. Suddenly, I knew that I did have the desire to continue as a coach, and that I wanted it as badly as ever. While the opportunity with Canada would have been one to relish, the chance to rebuild a team with so much untapped potential and such a proud tradition was one I could not turn down. I spoke with my family, put aside my lingering disappointment at the way things had turned out with New Zealand Rugby, and did what I knew in my heart I should do: I sent in my application to be head coach of the Samoan Sevens team.

After 22 years of coaching the New Zealand Sevens team and having all that pressure on my shoulders, I felt in a way that this was a new beginning. I was still driven by results, but I was able now to take on a team that shaped as a genuine project, rather than one that was, because of its historical success, expected to win every time it took the playing field. The challenge was not a new one; I simply had to put a high-performance programme in place that could build depth in the local ranks and entice the best Samoan talent abroad to return home for the chance to represent their nation. In this quest, I would have an immediate and familiar ally.

Alama Ieremia was no stranger to me. The 30-test All Black had once been a member of the New Zealand Sevens team and was the head coach of Manu Samoa. It was important for me to meet with him to gain an understanding of where the Samoan high-performance programme was at, and how we could work together to advance the causes of both the Manu Samoa side and the Samoan Sevens team. If we could work together with the same goals in mind, I knew we could create something truly special; I could develop the youngsters in the Samoan system who wanted to make their way through the ranks and into the Manu Samoa fifteens team, and Alama could help me understand the cultural nuances that would be important as I looked to imprint a new strategy on the sevens programme.

This symbiotic relationship was a bottom line for me if I was to take on the role and Alama understood why. Sevens had the opportunity to become the flagship for rugby in Samoa, and with proper care and custodianship, we could work together to offer young players a genuine pathway to international success. The high-performance venue in Apia had everything we needed – albeit shorn of some of the more exotic luxuries that players in other nations have at their disposal – and the two training fields at Apia Park and the Marist club were ideally suited to the rigours of sevens fitness work. In short, there was nothing to prevent us creating a team we believed could once again become a force to be reckoned with.

Officially, because of my existing contract with New Zealand Rugby, I wouldn't be able to start coaching the Samoan team until January of 2017, which was not an ideal situation for my prospective employer to have to face. However, as discussions continued, I began to feel as if this was the perfect job for me. I also knew that while I couldn't coach the team, I could begin to develop an understanding of what was required, and who I would be working with. I would be inheriting a side from the previous coaching team, one whose members I knew nothing about. It is imperative as a coach to gain an understanding of the people you will lead, and it had been something I had always done, both in rugby and in business. If you don't know where the buttons are, you'll never be able to push them. A sevens coach needs to be pushing all the buttons all the time.

There were more than 20 players from the previous year's programme who were still involved in the new campaign, not to mention the Samoan 'A' team members who I knew would offer us a ready-made platoon of potential players who could make the step up into the sevens side if they could prove to us that they were ready to perform. It was crucial to me to have someone like Stephen Betham, who had guided the Samoan Sevens side to their only World Series title in the 2009/10 series and who also led the Manu Samoa programme through to the 2015 Rugby World Cup, available to operate as an assistant coach. Talent identification was one of the most important aspects in coaching sevens, because the players who can deliver for you in the sport are often not the first, or most obvious, choices for fifteens coaches. Stephen lived locally, understood the club system and who the players were, and was enthusiastic about gaining an insight into the types of skill set I wanted to see in anyone I selected. There was, and is, no shortage of talent to choose from. Along with Stephen, I set about a journey of discovery through Samoan rugby.

———

Just like in Fiji, it feels as though every spare blade of grass in Samoa is being utilised for a pick-up game. On any drive through Apia you'll find kids engaged in active play on sports grounds, reserves and front yards. Whether it be rugby or touch or volleyball, there is a natural and wondrous inclination for physical pursuits in Samoa which explains both the athletic stature of those who come through the ranks and their incredible vision and skill level. New Zealanders believe that rugby is in our DNA, but if you have travelled through any of the islands you will understand that whatever genetic disposition towards the game we think we possess is nothing compared to what these kids are capable of utilising.

I knew I wouldn't have the financial resources I had during my time in New Zealand, but I genuinely felt that we had in place so many of the natural ingredients that would allow us to help get Samoa back into the top echelon of the Sevens World Series. On my early visits, and to this day, I was, and am, astounded at how welcoming the Samoan people have been. I was constantly surprised and not a little bit humbled when locals would stop to ask me why I would want to take on the job of coaching their team. The short answer is, because I wanted to. The long answer is a little more complicated.

The truth is, the Samoan people have a wealth of spirit, a

deep and abiding religious faith, and a culture of selflessness and generosity. However, by any Western measure of wellbeing, they are not so fortunate. It is a fact that many on the islands face financial hardship on a daily basis, and that sport is seen as a way to help not only the athlete but the entire family to overcome such a straitened existence. I can identify with the challenges that this lack of financial means can pose. My own upbringing was hardly the stuff of luxury, and when I paused to reflect on my childhood I felt a deep connection to the young athletes I met and to the many others that I would discover over time. Talent and perseverance can do so much that money never can.

My siblings and I were taught to appreciate the few things we had, and I see the same attributes in Samoa. Rugby in this tiny island nation may lack financial clout, but if we can learn first to appreciate and to cherish the players, then to reward them, we can begin to redress that imbalance. What I discovered on those earliest visits to Samoa as a potential head coach is this: if I could be seen to be helping, by pushing these players to greater heights, then they will go to whatever lengths they need to in order to repay that selection faith. That, I knew right from the start, would give me just as much joy as winning titles.

Having met with the administration of Samoan rugby, I also wanted to meet the players. If I was going to coach them, I needed to know who they were and how hard they were prepared to work. For us to be successful, the players had to buy in to what I believed was a high-performance team. They had to make shifts around how they trained, they had to make shifts about what they ate, and they had to be prepared to put in more effort than they had ever done before. If they weren't interested in buying in to all of those things, then we couldn't possibly hope to develop into a team that was capable of achieving anything.

There was something else: they had to be contracted to play. While that would prove the most difficult part of the process, my fervent belief was that we needed to put something on the table in order to retain the best players and to ensure that there would always be an experienced core who could in turn pass on their skills to the young players making their way through the system. Yes, talent and perseverance constituted the bedrock upon which the foundations of performance could be built, but at some point we needed to accept that we were part of a globalised professional game and as such had a choice: to be a perennial net exporter of our best players, or to offer some kind of financial reward to retain our talent.

As excited as I was by the idea of launching into a coaching role with Samoa, there was one other thing to deal with. After the disappointment of New Zealand's Olympic sevens campaign, I had to think long and hard about my approach, and whether I still trusted in what I had to offer as a coach. That personal evaluation was probably the most important element of all, given the way things had unravelled on the biggest stage the game had ever stood upon.

I had always maintained that I would never move away from things that have worked for me. After two decades in international coaching, you have to back yourself, and trust your instincts. That doesn't mean I am not constantly searching for innovative ways to take the team forward – fundamentally, sevens is a game of minute advantages – but I refuse to be caught up in what has become an industry that obsesses over fads. Yes, you win some and you lose some, yet too often in coaching and in life we use failure as a catalyst to discard all the things that worked, along with the things that did not.

I discussed this at length with the people I trusted the most – family, friends, my confidant and boss Warwick Talbut – and the conclusion was a simple one. If I took the job, I had to get back to the things that gave me purpose as a coach – namely, culture and conditioning. Once I got that culture instilled within the Samoan team, I sensed that they would be tough to beat. They are real athletes, driven to perform, and with all the skills and rugby intelligence required to shine on the global circuit. If I could impress upon them the need to buy in to that high-performance environment with 100 per cent commitment, the sky was the limit.

What makes a good coach and a good manager? People skills. It is the ability to earn the respect of the people you are in charge of. I believed from the very start that I had that respect from the Samoan players, and that gave me a massive boost. By contrast, I felt that over the previous 18 months in New Zealand some of that trust in me as a coach had been eroded, especially through the one-size-fits-all approach of New Zealand Rugby's High Performance team. For example, I maintained right to the last that the New Zealand Sevens team could not be treated like the All Blacks. The sevens game for me was different: conditioning and culture were the things that mattered. The All Blacks had a huge volume of players, whereas we had 12, and I think we lost sight of that. Everything is comparable to the All Blacks in New Zealand rugby, but that does not take into account the differences between the two sports.

In the most successful years for the New Zealand Sevens side it was all about doing the hard yards. That may not have been a universally popular approach, but to me it was the only way to keep getting the results we wanted to get. I do believe that over the last couple of seasons with the team those methods had come under greater scrutiny, and had been questioned more than ever before. Sevens as a sport required different thinking to fifteens, and in my opinion, it always had. The Samoan opportunity offered me the chance to get back to doing what I did best.

My first season in charge would be a challenging one, and I was prepared for that. I had gone from coaching a side that had never once missed the cup section of a tournament, to one that was struggling to make one. We had good days and some not so good days, but as the season unfolded I could see signs of life. I urged them to be patient, and to think about the next season, and the next step. That was the nature of sevens: one game at a time. It was always going to take some time for us to define our style and to grow our team but the commitment was there, the talent was there, and the desire to work hard shone through in all we did. That's all a coach can ask for at the end of the day: that you did your best. I knew, as far as results were concerned, the best was yet to come.

It was all about doing the hard yards. That may not have been a universally popular approach, but to me it was the only way to keep getting the results.

EPILOGUE
ON WITH IT

THERE WAS A lovely soft breeze that wafted in off the Pacific Ocean and through the window of my Apia hotel. It was refreshing in the heat, especially after a long day of meetings. It was July 2017 and I had just spent seven hours in air-conditioned offices sorting out travel, logistics, scheduling, accommodation, training programmes and everything else associated with the 2017/18 Sevens World Series. There were to be 12 events in total – 10 in the World Series, a World Cup, and a Commonwealth Games event on the Gold Coast. It is an incredibly complicated set-up, making sure the Samoan team has enough time at each venue, adequate breaks in between, and proper conditioning windows, especially for those in the side that will also be asked to help Samoa qualify for the 2019 Rugby World Cup in Japan. As yet, the team still hasn't managed to do that.

As I lay there, listening to the water and the sounds of Apia that drift in to my room on the breeze, I thought about 1994 and my first tournament in charge of New Zealand. We picked a team – at least, I picked a team – met for a week, flew to Hong Kong, won the cup and came home. That was that. One tournament and it was all over. How far this sport has come – how far I have come! – in the last 23 years! It sounds funny to say that number, 23. A part of me will forever remember that I was coach of the New Zealand team for 22 years. Now I have been coach of the Samoan team for one. After all this time around this game, around these great athletes, and in those vast stadia of the global series, packed to the gunnels with partygoers and serious fans alike, I can honestly say I have not tired of it at all. Not one bit. Seven hours in planning meetings I can probably do without, but that's the job. It has always been the job: making sure my team has the best chance to succeed at the highest level. I can build the culture, and I can condition my players to be sevens fit, but I need everything to run smoothly so they can focus solely on playing the game.

I've spent some time thinking about this shift, about the way things finished up in New Zealand, and I have no regrets. I was able to live out my coaching dreams with that side, and for 22 years as well. Plenty of great people helped me out along the way, and what a gift to have spent time with the players in that team. Some are sadly no longer with us – Joe Tauiwi, Norm Berryman, Jonah Lomu. All of them are missed. I got to see them at their very best, when they had youth on their side, fire in their bellies (or nothing at all, as Norm might quip), and an adoring crowd watching them tear it up at the most iconic tournament of all. I watched my captain Eric Rush nurture that big Jonah kid. I don't think enough is made of the fact that, without Eric, there may never have been Jonah as the world came to recognise him. Eric would likely call bullshit on that, but that's just because he's a humble man who never expected an ounce of credit for the 17 seasons he spent giving his all for his country on the sports field. He has probably made it all back now, anyway. He's certainly done enough after-dinner speaking!

Eric Rush and Dallas Seymour stand out as two of the greatest sporting leaders this country has ever produced. Their integrity and ability to find humour in the horror of training never ceased to amaze me. They were honest, upfront, unyielding on the field, and truly respectful of the jersey and grateful for their opportunities. I could never have wished for better leaders. I had other fine captains too, among them DJ Forbes who put the pride back into New Zealand sevens. He left his mark, too, in his own quiet and unassuming way.

There were so many characters in all those years. Players who still make me laugh just thinking about them. I remember having to turn one guy around during shuttles on the field at Blake Park in Mount Maunganui. He was so exhausted he couldn't remember which way he was supposed to go. I eventually just let him run off into the distance. I couldn't pick him. How could I pick a guy who didn't know which way he was running?

There were tough moments, too. Moments when you had to let someone down. I had always tried to do that in a positive way. I never wanted to shut the door on someone forever. I learned over the years that all the best intentions do little to salve a wounded pride, or fix a shattered dream. Those meetings, those conversations, they were always hard for me, but I know now that they were much harder on the other guy. I will have to make more of those decisions, of course. That's a coach's job. It's about the only thing I will not be looking forward to this year.

It is going to take some serious work ahead to get Samoa back to the top level in world sevens, but there is the will here. I can sense it when I talk to the players and when I watch them sweat in the afternoon sun at Apia Park or on the fields at the Marist club. They remind me so much of the early teams I took in New Zealand. They grit their teeth and they get through the work, and then they laugh their arses off. It feels like home.

There is something about Samoa that reminds me of my childhood. The people are courteous, respectful, gracious and vibrant. The kids play outside on sunny afternoons. They have pick-up games of rugby and endless volleyball contests. Everywhere is a restless energy, everywhere is an athlete to be discovered, a talent to be nurtured. For the last year I have been around the island and with Samoan players around the world, searching for that X-factor, that one point of difference. In other words, I have been doing exactly what I was doing before. It's a different country but the same rules apply. Find the players, set the expectations: culture and conditioning.

There had been glimpses in my first year in charge of the team, peeps at the potential in the side. While we had only managed one cup semifinal appearance in that 2016/17 season, we knew we had games that were ours for the taking. It was the finest of lines some days, but that's what this sport is all about. You tread that line between perfection and dejection every time you take the field. In fifteens rugby, you have time for luck to work its way back to even in the course of a game. Both teams will get their chance at the lucky bounce. In sevens, there is no time for that. One bounce, one chance that isn't taken – that's the difference between winning games, if not tournaments.

It was crucial that we stayed positive as a team. With such an important year ahead, it was all about focusing on the things we can improve: learning to trust our instinct for the game and our team-mates to go out there and do what needs to be done. We have a powerful team, one that can tip up any nation on its day. We just have to have that day, and we will. This team will only get fitter and better. The natural skills, the athleticism, the individual points of difference will all emerge from there. That is what you aim for as a sevens coach – to take that raw talent and enable it to shine.

Many people in Samoa still talk to me about the Samoan team that won the World Series in 2009/10. It was a wonderful team, filled with game breakers and pace, players who could work their magic at will, and players who could punish ball carriers with their defence. There's no reason the next wave of Samoan talent cannot emerge from the long shadow cast by names like Mikaele Pesamino, Reupena Levasa, Afa Aiono and, of course, the great Uale Mai. That generation of Samoan players was lethal. This generation can be as well.

In many ways, it gives me a great sense of purpose to be here with the Samoan team. New Zealand rugby, and certainly the sevens team, owes so much to the Pacific nations. So many of our players came through Samoan programmes on their way through to represent New Zealand, and they could just as easily have done the same for their native country. We were blessed to have them, and I wonder how things may have been different if we had not. For every boy who came to school in New Zealand and found themselves on New Zealand Rugby's watch list, there are hundreds more who have just as much talent, and who could aspire to play sevens for Samoa. That search is still on. It's funny how it never stops.

There is trust here in Samoa. I know the players have bought in to the programme that Stephen and I have set for them. There is no getting away from the testing and the running. There are shifts to be made in team nutrition and education around high-performance diets. There will be the appointment of a full-time strength and conditioning coach, too. We advertised the job in the middle of 2017 and were immediately flooded with CVs from around the world. Sevens is an Olympic sport now, after all. And besides, who wouldn't want to spend time in Samoa?

In my first year in charge in 2017, my son Paul, nowadays a physical education teacher and the coach of the Bay of Plenty men's sevens team, helped me with the side for the last four tournaments of the season. It was a time to cherish. To know that my son has followed in my footsteps and that he can offer so much to teams through his knowledge and passion for the game is very pleasing. I did wonder at times whether my children thought they were missing out with their father being away so often, but to know that they have followed every step of this journey with me and, in Paul's case now, shared a few steps of it, too, gives me a tremendous sense of accomplishment.

When a sevens team is playing at peak condition, you just know every pass is going to find their hands, every kick is going to bounce into their hands, every tackle is going to be made, and every chance is going to be finished off. When you see a team with the fitness to match the skills, I do not think there is a more enchanting or explosive sport on the planet. Whenever I head back to Samoa for a camp, I picture that kind of performance. That is what we are always searching for as coaches. That is why we hover at ground level, wanting to feel each tackle and listen to the chat. We want to see the space being created, and the jaws clenched, and the strain on the faces. And we want to see those tries that start

90 metres downfield and involve every player in the team. That's when the game is at its most dynamic and beautiful. That's what I want to see from Samoa.

Will it take time? Of course it will. I do hope there is patience. I know in my heart that with the right people around the team, we can help Samoa become a force once more. We can see them winning World Series titles and who knows what else. Promisingly for the sport in Samoa, I can see the next generation of stars already performing on the big stage. In 2017, rugby sevens was part of the Commonwealth Youth Games in the Bahamas. Samoa, with just one pool loss across the three days of the tournament, won through to face England in the gold-medal match. They had already beaten England in pool play, and they would emerge triumphant once more in the final.

It was a moment to savour for those young men, and for Samoan sevens. In the build-up to the event, they had come under the watch of Stephen Betham, my assistant coach with the national team, and a veteran coach himself. In order to give the team the best chance of success in the Bahamas, Steve focused on their fitness. I must say it was pleasing to know that after everything that has happened in the last 23 years of coaching, some things really have never changed. In order to get that champion team firing for the Commonwealth Youth Games, Steve had one tool up his sleeve. I chuckled when he told me what the fitness sessions consisted of.

'The usual,' he said, 'sixteen one-hundred-and-fifty-metre shuttles with forty seconds' rest.'

I thought that was about the most encouraging thing I had heard in a very long time.

BY THE NUMBERS
SIR GORDON TIETJENS AND
THE NEW ZEALAND SEVENS TEAM

WIN/LOSS RECORDS IN ALL YEARS

YEAR	TOURNAMENTS	WINS	LOSSES	PTS FOR	PTS AGAINST
1994	1	5	0	183	51
1995	5	19	3	655	172
1996	5	27	2	1263	236
1997	3	12	3	442	211
1998	5	24	3	1006	207
1999	10	49	4	1670	426
2000	10	55	4	2048	354
2001	10	56	4	2042	330
2002	13	68	6	2377	565
2003	7	34	6	1285	411
2004	8	39	7	1396	395
2005	8	41	7	1509	441
2006	9	36	10	1380	551
2007	8	40	4	1391	355
2008	8	43	4	1350	367
2009	9	37	12	1262	514
2010	9	43	7	1531	541
2011	9	43	7	1479	519
2012	9	46	8	1375	556
2013	10	52	8	1651	584
2014	10	50	10	1645	511
2015	8	33	13	1039	692
2016	9	39	10	1142	691
TOTAL	**183**	**891 (86%)**	**142**	**31,121**	**9680**

TOURNAMENT VICTORIES

1994 Hong Kong Sevens

1995 Argentina International Sevens; Hong Kong Sevens; Japan International Sevens

1996 Uruguay International Sevens; Hong Kong Sevens; World Cup Qualifier, Portugal

1998 Japan Sevens; XVI Commonwealth Games

1999 Uruguay Sevens; Argentina Sevens; Chile Sevens; Sydney Sevens; Japan Sevens; Paris Sevens; Dubai Sevens

2000 Uruguay Sevens; Fiji Sevens; Hong Kong Sevens; Paris Sevens; South Africa Sevens; Dubai Sevens

2001 Rugby World Cup Sevens, Argentina; Hong Kong Sevens; Japan Sevens; London Sevens; Wales Sevens; Dubai Sevens; South Africa Sevens

2002 Chile Sevens; China Sevens; Singapore Sevens; Malaysian Sevens; England Sevens; Wales Sevens; XVII Commonwealth Games; Dubai Sevens

2003 New Zealand Sevens

2004 New Zealand Sevens; France Sevens; South Africa Sevens

2005 New Zealand Sevens; Los Angeles Sevens; Singapore Sevens

2006 XVIII Commonwealth Games; South Africa Sevens

2007 England Sevens; Scotland Sevens; Dubai Sevens; South Africa Sevens

2008 New Zealand Sevens; USA Sevens; Hong Kong Sevens; Scotland Sevens;

2009 Dubai Sevens; South Africa Sevens

2010 XIX Commonwealth Games; South Africa Sevens

2011 New Zealand Sevens; Hong Kong Sevens; Australia Sevens; South Africa Sevens

2012 New Zealand Sevens; Scotland Sevens; South Africa Sevens

2013 England Sevens: Australia Sevens; Rugby World Cup Sevens

2014 New Zealand Sevens; Hong Kong Sevens; Scotland Sevens; England Sevens

2015 New Zealand Sevens

2016 New Zealand Sevens; Australia Sevens; Canada Sevens

WORLD SERIES TITLES

Series contested: 17

Series Championships: 12

Series Runners up: 1

Series Third place: 2

COMMONWEALTH GAMES

Tournaments contested: 5

Gold Medals: 4

Silver Medals: 1

PLAYER LIST

Below is a list of all the sevens players who represented New Zealand during Sir Gordon Tietjens' tenure as coach. Dates indicate the year each player made their sevens debut, and an asterisk marks all those who had also played or went on to play for the All Blacks (fifteen-a-side) as at 22 September 2017. This list was compiled with the help of Clive Akers.

EJ (Eric) Rush, 1988 *
DJ (Dallas) Seymour, 1988 *
MSL (Scott) Pierce, 1989
GTM (Graeme) Bachop, 1990 *
GM (Glen) Osborne, 1992 *
PGA (Peter) Woods, 1993
KT (Kyle) Bruning, 1994
L (Luke) Erenavula, 1994
MT (Martin) Jones, 1994
JJ (Joe) Tauiwi, 1994
AR (Aaron) Hamilton, 1994
JT (Jonah) Lomu, 1994 *
CD (Carl) Murray, 1994
AR (Adrian) Cashmore, 1995 *
AF (Andrew) Blowers, 1995 *
RQ (Roger) Randle, 1995 *
OJ (Owen) Scrimgeour, 1995
J (Joeli) Vidiri, 1995 *
CM (Christian) Cullen, 1995 *
BRM (Bradley) Fleming, 1995

TK (Tony) Maidens, 1995
CS (Caleb) Ralph, 1996 *
DT (Damien) Karauna, 1996
W (Waisake) Masirewa, 1996
GM (Greg) Peacocke, 1996
DA (Donald) Smith, 1996
OW (Ora) John, 1996
KJ (Kirk) Wotherspoon, 1996
EM (Eugene) Martin, 1996
KS (Karl) Tenana, 1996
TR (Rua) Tipoki, 1997
A (Alama) Ieremia, 1997 *
NR (Norman) Berryman, 1997 *
RJL (Rhys) Duggan, 1997 *
AJ (Andrew) Miller, 1997
A (Aisea) Tuilevu, 1997
TV (Troy) Flavell, 1998 *
AC (Tony) Monaghan, 1998
PT (Paul) Schmidt-Uili, 1998
T (Tauna'holo) Taufahema, 1998

BM (Blair) Foote, 1998
RL (Rico) Gear, 1998 *
SI (Sam) Nonoa, 1998
DT (Dan) Parkinson, 1998
JT Thomas, 1998
A (Amasio) Valence, 1998
BT (Bruce) Reihana, 1998 *
CD (Craig) De Goldi, 1998
TH (Trevor) Savou, 1998
O (Orene) A'ii, 1999
SJ (Jared) Going, 1999
JC (Justin) Wilson, 1999
CS (Carl) Izatt, 1999
PC (Paul) Steinmetz, 1999 *
HSE (Shayne) Austin, 1999
C (Craig) Hudson, 1999
CA (Craig) Newby, 1999 *
MT (Matua) Parkinson, 1999
M (Massey) Tuhakaraina, 1999
LS (Luke) Andrews, 1999
TG (Todd) Blythe, 1999
JM (Mils) Muliaina, 1999 *
BD (Brendon) Haami, 2000
JA (Jason) Tiatia, 2000
HRI (Hayden) Martine, 2000
R (Rodney) So'oialo, 2000 *
DSM (Donovan) Nepia, 2000
JJ (Johnny) Leo'o, 2000
KMT (Kristian) Ormsby, 2000
TSJ (Tafai) Ioasa, 2001
MC (Chris) Masoe, 2001 *
NI (Nick) Collins, 2001
RE (Ross) Martin, 2001
HB (Hayden) Reid, 2001

MR (Mana) Ashford, 2001
SKM (Sione) Kepu, 2001
K (Kevin) Senio, 2001
AM (Alan) Bunting, 2002
NJ (Nick) Evans, 2002 *
A (Tony) Koonwaiyou, 2002
JM (Josh) Blackie, 2002
JT (Joe) Rokocoko, 2002 *
ASM (Anthony) Tuitavake, 2002 *
CB (Chris) Smylie, 2002
RU (Roy) Kinikinilau, 2002
LJ (Liam) Messam, 2002 *
I (Ilisea) Tanivula, 2002
NA (Nathaniel) Walker, 2002
BWT (Bryan) Milne, 2002
SL (Scott) Waldrom, 2002 *
CNO (Charles) Baxter, 2003
GA (Grant) Webb, 2003
HE (Hosea) Gear, 2003 *
LO (Lifeimi) Mafi, 2003
GA (Grant) McQuoid, 2004
RN (Rudi) Wulf, 2004 *
TD (Tanerau) Latimer, 2004 *
CR (Colin) Bourke, 2004
SR (Sosene) Anesi, 2004 *
MA (Ma'a) Nonu, 2004 *
SL (Sherwin) Stowers, 2004
E (Edwin) Cocker, 2005
I (Isaia) Toeava, 2005 *
TE (Tamati) Ellison, 2005 *
M (Marc) Camburn, 2005
N (Nigel) Hunt, 2005
J (Jason) Hona, 2005
BA (Brent) Wilson, 2005

GE (George) Naoupu, 2005

T (Tomasi) Cama, 2005

VM (Viliami) Waqaseduadua, 2005

J (Jerome) Kaino, 2005 *

RM (Mark) Ranby, 2005 *

LJT (Lance) MacDonald, 2005

ZW (Zar) Lawrence, 2005

HL (Hayden) Pedersen, 2005

A (Alfred) Pelenise, 2005

JT (James) Maher, 2006

A (Alando) Soakai, 2006

DWH (Dwayne) Sweeney, 2006

CS (Cory) Jane, 2006 *

L (Lote) Raikabula, 2006

OJ (Onosai) Tololima-Auva'a, 2006

DJ Forbes, 2006

LH (Lachie) Munro, 2006

TP (Tu) Umaga-Marshall, 2006

A (Asipeli) Dauwai, 2006

PSV (Solomon) King, 2006

JMRA (Jarrad) Hoeata, 2006 *

RMN (Rene) Ranger, 2006 *

WTC (Willie) Rickards, 2006

NJ (Nick) Thomson, 2006

SP (Steven) Yates, 2007

AJ (Adam) Thomson, 2007 *

BAC (Ben) Atiga, 2007 *

VVJ (Victor) Vito, 2007 *

IJA (Israel) Dagg, 2007 *

TJKJ (James) Kamana, 2007

TJ (Tim) Mikkelson, 2007

NH (Nafi) Tuitavake, 2008

CK (Chad) Tuoro, 2008

KG (Kendrick) Lynn, 2008

BC (Ben) Nowell, 2008

D (David) Smith, 2008

SJ (Julian) Savea, 2008 *

TT (Tim) Nanai-Williams, 2008

KT (Kurt) Baker, 2008

PW (Paul) Grant, 2008

A (Alex) Tulou, 2008

S (Save) Tokula, 2009

BJ (Ben) Souness, 2009

JR (Jordan) Puletua, 2009

LG (Luke) Hamilton, 2009

FT (Tutu) Tairea, 2009

TC (Toby) Arnold, 2009

B (Buxton) Popoali'i, 2009

FA (Fritz) Lee, 2010

T (Leka) Tupuola, 2010

BJ (Beauden) Barrett, 2010 *

BR (Ben) Smith, 2010 *

ZR (Zac) Guildford, 2010 *

F (Frank) Halai, 2010 *

DPT (Declan) O'Donnell, 2010

JT (Jackson) Ormond, 2010

SB (Scott) Curry, 2010

BI (Bryce) Heem, 2010

JB (Jack) McPhee, 2010

DA (David) Raikuna, 2011

RJL (Rory) Grice, 2011

SA (Shane) Christie, 2011

ST (Charles) Piutau, 2011 *

TJ (Joe) Webber, 2011

JR (James) Marshall, 2011

GA (Glen) Robertson, 2011

KFT (Kylem) O'Donnell, 2011

G (George) Tilsley, 2011

MB (Mark) Jackman, 2012

AS (Ardie) Savea, 2012 *

WR (Waisake) Naholo, 2012 *

JR (Johnathan) Malo, 2012

L (Lolagi) Visinia, 2012

JH (Jack) Wilson, 2012

WH (Warwick) Lahmert, 2012

GD (Gareth) Williams Spiers, 2012

JA (Jamie) Verran, 2012

B (Belgium) Tuatagaloa, 2012

I (Iopu) Ipou, 2012

RAM (Rhys) Llewellyn, 2012

MB (Ben) Lam, 2012

SN (Sam) Dickson, 2012

MM (Milford) Keresoma, 2012

LR (Luke) Masirewa, 2013

RN (Rocky) Khan, 2013

GG (Gillies) Kaka, 2013

TA (Trinity) Spooner-Neera, 2013

MA (Matt) Faddes, 2013

PJ (Pita) Ahki, 2013

AAD (Ambrose) Curtis, 2013

AL (Akira) Ioane, 2014

MR (Marty) McKenzie, 2014

AJ (Adam) Whitelock, 2014

AC (Tony) Ensor, 2014

MJ (Matt) Clutterbuck, 2014

MVU (Murphy) Taramai, 2014

ST (Sam) Vaka, 2014

RE (Rieko) Ioane, 2015 *

BRT (Beaudein) Waaka, 2015

EJ (Jack) Goodhue, 2015

DJ (Dylan) Collier, 2015

LH (Lewis) Ormond, 2015

FJ (Jordan) Bunce, 2015

IR (Isaac) Te Tamaki, 2015

RE (Regan) Ware, 2015

AW (Augustine) Pulu, 2015 *

MB (Max) Pearson, 2015

AI (Antonio) Kiri Kiri, 2015

TZBP (Teddy) Stanaway, 2015

SW (Sonny-Bill) Williams, 2016 *

SLJ (Sione) Molia, 2016

JJA (Josh) Van Lieshout, 2016

IN (Isaac) Te Aute, 2016

ACKNOWLEDGEMENTS

I HAVE BEEN truly blessed in this life to have been able to follow my passion. For more than a quarter of a century I have been able to call myself a coach, and what an amazing and rewarding experience that has been. Whatever I have achieved personally has only been possible because of the people who have supported my dreams, and I am truly indebted to you all.

I would like to dedicate this book, first and foremost, to my wife Jules. You have been there in good times and through many challenges that were not of your own making. You never once wavered in your love and encouragement and positivity. Thank you for the power that has given me.

To my children, Paul and Kylie, I thank you for your patience and unconditional love. Coaching internationally means many months away from home, and you never begrudged me that. To my brothers and sister, and the rest of my extended family, a big thanks for being there always. To my wonderful circle of friends, thanks for looking out for us all.

New Zealand Rugby gave me the opportunity of a lifetime many years ago, and I am sincerely grateful. It was not always smooth sailing, but without your belief in me, this story would never have been written for this amazing life would never have been lived.

To every member of my teams – both management and players – I say this: through all these years you have collectively risen to the challenge and have consistently achieved success on the world stage. You should be so proud of what you have done through your dedication and hard work. I cherish you all.

SPECIAL ACKNOWLEDGEMENTS

To Warwick and Lesley Talbut and your family, I don't know what to say other than this: your continued and frankly unbelievable support for me over such a long period of time has been life-changing.

To all at Bay Engineers Supplies: what a team!

Gary Chapman at Emirates, and his wife Penny; Petra-Lee and the team at Sidetrack Café, Mt Maunganui; everyone at Oceanside Resort & Twin Towers, Mt Maunganui – thanks to you all for your tremendous care and support over the years.

Finally, I would like to thank Scotty Stevenson for his time in writing this book, which required endless hours of research. I also want to thank him for his passion and enthusiasm for the sevens game.

Sir Gordon Tietjens
September 2017

ABOUT THE CO-AUTHOR

SCOTTY STEVENSON is a writer and broadcaster who has covered New Zealand's national game since 2007. He has followed rugby at all levels both domestically and internationally and has also reported on the Olympic Games, Olympic Winter Games and Commonwealth Games. He is a regular columnist and feature writer and has previously written biographies of All Blacks Cory Jane and Stephen 'Beaver' Donald, and renowned rowers Hamish Bond and Eric Murray.

Scotty continues to work for SKY Sport as a rugby commentator and presenter, and contributes to a range of media outlets as a weekly columnist. He lives in Auckland with his wife Claire and sons Ethan and Joe.

CO-AUTHOR'S NOTE

SIR GORDON TIETJENS managed to coach the New Zealand Sevens team for a staggering 22 years. Quite what drove him to do that was beyond me, until I sat down with him to get to grips with the secret to his longevity and success. What I discovered was a mind equally as comfortable in the business world as it is on the rugby field. I also discovered that his story is really about the pursuit of excellence and what it takes to catch up.

Sir Gordon's 12 World Series titles, four Commonwealth Games gold medals, and two World Cups are the tangible rewards for a career that has shaped the game of sevens as we know it today, but they do not tell us about what motivated him or how he went about creating his unrivalled legacy. I wanted this record of his life in coaching to be a guidebook for success in any endeavour. I am much obliged to him for allowing me to help tell his story. I am also thankful to Peter White for the set-up; to Jeremy Sherlock for his patience; and to Claire, Ethan, Joe and Judy for everything.

Finally, to all the players past, present and future, you'll be pleased to know that he didn't break me.

Scotty Stevenson
August 2017

PENGUIN

UK | USA | Canada | Ireland | Australia
India | New Zealand | South Africa | China

Penguin is an imprint of the Penguin Random House
group of companies, whose addresses can be found
at global.penguinrandomhouse.com.

Penguin
Random House
New Zealand

First published by Penguin Random House New Zealand, 2017

1 3 5 7 9 10 8 6 4 2

Text © Sir Gordon Tietjens, 2017
Photography © as credited, 2017

The moral right of Scotty Stevenson to be identified
as the author has been asserted.

All rights reserved. Without limiting the rights under copyright reserved above, no part
of this publication may be reproduced, stored in or introduced into a retrieval system, or
transmitted, in any form or by any means (electronic, mechanical, photocopying, recording
or otherwise), without the prior written permission of both the copyright owner and the
above publisher of this book.

Design by Rachel Clark © Penguin Random House New Zealand
Typesetting by Cat Taylor © Penguin Random House New Zealand
Cover photograph by Justin Arthur/Photosport
Prepress by Image Centre Group
Printed and bound in Australia by Griffin Press,
an Accredited ISO AS/NZS 14001 Environmental Management Systems Printer

A catalogue record for this book is available
from the National Library of New Zealand.

ISBN 978-0-14-377161-6
eISBN 978-0-14-377162-3

penguin.co.nz